INNOVATIONS IN DEVELOPMENT FINANCE

The Council of State Planning Agencies is a membership organization comprised of the planning and policy staff of the nation's governors. Through its Washington office, the Council provides assistance to individual states on a wide spectrum of policy matters. The Council also performs policy and technical research on both state and national issues. The Council was formed in 1966; it became affiliated with The National Governors' Association in 1975.

In addition to *Studies in State Development Policy,* the Council publishes:

■ *CSPA Working Papers.* Current volumes address: environmental protection and economic development; commercial bank financing for small business enterprise; the investment of public pension funds; venture capital and urban development; the impact of regional shopping malls; the operation of minority capital markets; and the public service costs of alternative development patterns. A full list of current volumes is available on request.

■ *State Planning Issues.* A journal concerning the problems and practice of planning in the states. Published twice yearly.

■ *The State Planning Series.* Sixteen short papers dealing with financial management, citizen participation, econometrics, urban and rural development, policy development techniques, multi-state organizations, federal-state partnerships, and other issues of concern to state officials.

To order *Studies in State Development Policy* see page 167.

The Council of State Planning Agencies
Hall of the States
444 North Capitol Street
Washington, D.C. 20001
(202) 624-5386

Robert N. Wise
Director

Michael Barker
Associate Director for
Community and Economic Development

INNOVATIONS IN DEVELOPMENT FINANCE

LAWRENCE LITVAK
BELDEN DANIELS

COVER: "Map 1963," by Jasper Johns. Collection Albert Saalsfield. Grateful acknowledgement is made to Mr. Johns for allowing the reproduction of his work.

Partial funding support for this volume was received from the Office of Economic Research, Economic Development Administration, the U.S. Department of Commerce. The views and findings it contains are the author's, and do not necessarily represent those of the Economic Development Administration or the members or staff of The Council of State Planning Agencies. Reproduction of any part of this volume is permitted for any purpose of the United States Government.

Copyright © 1979 by The Council of State Planning Agencies, Hall of the States, 444 North Capitol Street, Washington, D.C. 20001.

Library of Congress Catalog Number: 79-67381

ISBN: 0-93482-02-7

Printed in the United States of America. First printing - 1979.

Format conceptualization and series coordination: Katherine Kinsella
Design: Kathy Jungjohann
Typesetting and Layout: Teri Grimwood
Printing and binding services: George Banta Co.

TABLE OF CONTENTS

PREFACE .... *ix*

EXECUTIVE SUMMARY *1*

1 FACING REALITY *11*
   The Limited Role of Capital.............................*11*
   Who Gets Capital and Why *17*
   The Significance of Capital Market Failure...............*24*
   Summary *25*

**2 STATE POLICIES
AND ECONOMIC DEVELOPMENT** *27*
   Tax Policy *27*
   Expenditure Policy....................................*30*
   Regulatory Policy *32*
   Summary *34*

3 THE CAPITAL AVAILABILITY PROBLEM *36*
   *Effect of Capital Market Imperfections
on Key Sources of Employment Growth* *36*
   Housing Finance.....................................*52*
   Public Infrastructure Finance..........................*54*

**4 GOALS AND TOOLS: FORMS OF STATE
INTERVENTION IN CAPITAL MARKETS** *58*
   Asking the Right Questions *58*
   From Questions to Answers *61*
   *Administrative Regulation
of State Financial Intermediaries*.......................*61*
   *Influencing Financial Intermediaries
Through Economic Incentives* *66*
   Direct State Financial Intermediation...................*71*

**5 OPTIONS FOR FINANCING BUSINESS
ENTERPRISE: INFLUENCING PRIVATE
FINANCIAL MARKETS AND INSTITUTIONS** *77*

*Using State Regulatory Authority
to Influence Private Capital Flows* 77

*Using Economic Incentives to Influence
Private Capital Flows* 90

**6 OPTIONS FOR FINANCING BUSINESS
ENTERPRISE: CREATING STATE-OWNED
FINANCIAL INTERMEDIARIES** 99

Debt Intermediaries Financed Through Bonds 99

Debt Intermediaries Financed Through Tax Revenue 107

Equity-Providing Intermediaries 110

*State and Local Public Funds
As a Source of Development Capital* 118

**7 OPTIONS FOR FINANCING HOUSING
AND INFRASTRUCTURE** 126

Financing Housing 127

Financing Public Infrastructure 138

8 TARGETING CAPITAL TO COMMUNITIES 144

*Geographically Targeting Capital
Availability for Underfinanced Enterprises* 146

*Compensating for Locational Disadvantages
Through Capital Subsidies* 149

The Special Problem of Retaining Mature Firms 152

*Maximizing the Benefits of Depressed Area
Development* 154

BIBLIOGRAPHY 161

PREFACE

This study looks at how state governments can use policies directed at capital markets to enhance state economic development. It is part of the series, *Studies in State Development Policy,* commissioned by the Council of State Planning Agencies under a grant from the U.S. Economic Development Administration.

While this study has been prepared primarily for policymakers in state government, it contains information relevant to anyone concerned about how states and communities can exert greater control over their economic destinies.

Four major issues are analyzed:

- What is the role of capital in state economic development?
- When do capital markets fail to make funds available to the enterprises which can use them most productively?
- How can state governments influence the allocation of capital?
- How well have specific capital market policies at the state level performed?

Our analysis draws upon a variety of evidence, including academic studies, state government documents, interviews, and direct experience with several development finance programs.

EXECUTIVE SUMMARY

I. Increasing Capital Supply Or Reducing Capital Costs Will Not Necessarily Save Firms, Or Regions.

Profound world economic forces and federal government actions constrain the ability of states to affect economic activity through policies of any kind, let alone capital market ones.

The cost of capital is relatively small in the overall costs of doing business, and the availability of capital is a necessary but often insufficient factor. The demand for capital by enterprises in a state, and the corresponding attractiveness of a state for investment, depend primarily on whether it has a growing market and on its supply of resources other than capital.

But simply because capital does not lead the way does not mean that well-functioning capital markets are not a critical enabling factor in state economic development. On the contrary, opportunities for employment and income growth may go unrealized when capital markets fail to channel funds to enterprises that could use them most productively. And even well-functioning capital markets, left to their own devices, will not finance investment projects that fail to offer a competitive private return but provide compensating social benefits.

II. Capital-Related Policies Need To Be Part Of A Larger State Effort.

If states can influence their economic futures at all, it will be through a combination of long-term taxation, expenditure and regulatory policies.

In analyzing these three vehicles for potential state economic development policy, it is clear that many of the policies states currently pursue are simply wrongheaded. Lowering business taxes and providing tax incentives, it turns out, makes little difference in business location decisions, yet states consistently compete with each other to give away scarce taxpayer dollars. On the other hand, a coherent state expenditure and regulatory policy can make a whole state more attractive, and can have a significant influence on where economic activity takes place within the state.

We stress the *judicious* use of these instruments to stimulate economic development. More jobs and higher per capita money incomes are not the only, or necessarily the primary, goals of state policy. State governments must also be concerned about working conditions, the environment, and the needs of those people whom development passes by.

III. States Should Recognize The Capital Availability Problem That Impedes The Growth Of Job-Generating, Small Firms.

Although branch plants and subsidiaries generate a significant amount of employment, the birth and expansion of independent single plant firms is equally important to job creation. It is precisely these small firms that are most likely to have difficulty gaining access to capital because of imperfections in capital markets.

These are the firms that suffer from inadequate mechanisms for spreading and pooling risk, unduly high information and transaction costs, various forms of prejudice, market concentration, and the perverse consequences of some federal and state government regulation of capital markets. On the whole, small firms have higher debt/equity ratios, reflecting their difficulty in raising equity capital, through either the public market or venture capitalists. Their debt financing differs as well, being shorter in term and when long term, more often from banks as opposed to private placement sources.

States must also look at the role of housing and infrastructure in creating markets, jobs and a climate for growing economic enterprise, and at capital market imperfections that may impede the development of supportive housing and infrastructure.

IV. There Are Two Basic Approaches To Intervention In The Development Process Through Capital Market Policies.

First, if a state can counteract or correct the problems that produce underfinancing of viable small business, housing and public infrastructure projects, then additional employment and income growth will occur in the state.

Second, in theory, the cost of capital can be depressed to balance out other production costs or market disadvantages in a state or substate area. Thus even though the cost of capital normally does not represent an important determinant of where job-creating investment takes place, it might be manipulated to influence industrial location. Both practical and political considerations, however, may severely limit the usefulness of this approach in American states.

Whether making capital available to underfinanced firms or reducing its costs to others, a state is faced with altering the normal operation of private capital markets. In doing so it has three alternatives. It can influence the allocation and pricing of capital by existing private financial intermediaries through its power to regulate these institutions. It can influence this behavior through offering certain economic incentives. Or the state can establish state owned and controlled financial intermediaries designed to make the desired financing directly.

Effective state economic development policy causes jobs and incomes to be created when they would not otherwise be. Any policy that proposes to accomplish this feat—including those operating through capital markets—should be subjected to several questions. Since the policy intends to add employment, where do the jobs come from? What does the policy cost? What are the most appropriate tools for triggering the jobs? How well has the policy performed in other places? How might it be improved upon?

V. Both Administrative Regulation And Economic Incentives Can Be Used To Influence The Investment Behavior Of Private Financial Intermediaries And Individual Investors.

Historically, regulation of state-chartered, private financial intermediaries has given short shrift to the objective of fostering state economic development. States can use three types of financial regulation: Liability regulations affect the sources of funds, asset regulations affect the uses of funds, and market structure regulations affect the chartering and branching of financial institutions.

■ The most direct regulatory vehicles for influencing the availability or cost of capital are rules governing asset holdings. However, if required loans or investments are either riskier or less profitable than assets in the current portfolios of financial intermediaries, then the regulation may act like a tax. Those subject to the requirement will press for its removal, threatening that capital will flow away from state-chartered financial institutions to federally chartered ones in the state, or from the state as a whole to places not subject to that form of asset regulation. The threat is a credible one. While the power of a state government ends at its borders, the flow of capital does not observe these same boundaries. On the contrary, financial capital is quite mobile.

■ Although asset regulation would seem to be a much more direct way to influence who gets access to capital, in fact, liability regulation has a significant indirect impact. The reason is simple, the uses of funds are constrained by the sources of funds. As a general proposition, loosening restrictions on the price, term and nature of liabilities will increase competition between classes of financial institutions and encourage them to look for more creative ways to lend or invest their assets.

■ In exercising its authority to charter financial institutions, the state acts as a gatekeeper for the supply side of capital markets. This authority might be used to charter new, special purpose, private financial institutions that would fill gaps in the existing institutional networks. However, previous efforts in this area—so-called Business Development Corporations—have not been well designed.

■ Finally, state government restrictions on where a bank may branch supposedly protect the public; they in fact contribute substantially to monopoly and oligopoly banking market conditions that restrict the availability of credit, particularly to smaller enterprises. This represents a ripe area for regulatory change.

One response to the limits of an administrative regulatory approach is a strategy that acknowledges that the driving force of private capital flows in the economy is the pursuit of profit. Such an approach attempts to harness private investment to public purposes by creating incentives for financial institutions and other investors to channel capital in the right direction.

■ In practice, economic incentives have usually been employed to induce firms to locate or expand in one state as opposed to another. Any state considering lowering capital costs as an incentive to stimulate investment should be aware of several serious obstacles. Interstate and interregional production cost and market differences can be substantial. Capital subsidies, to be effective, may have to be very large and quite expensive. Moreover, unless the state can predict very accurately the cases where a subsidy will make a difference, a lot of money will be wasted giving subsidies to firms that would have invested anyway. We recommend subsidies only be given where strong evidence can be presented that the investment will not be made otherwise, subsidies can be kept proportionate to job and income benefits, and there is full public disclosure of subsidies and offsetting benefits.

■ In contrast to capital subsidies, state loan guarantee programs represent a promising but fairly undeveloped economic incentive policy. Their promise lies in a capacity to attract capital from banks and other investors for certain viable business opportunities in a state's economy that private financial institutions have not taken advantage of for a variety of reasons. We recommend that states adopting this tool establish eligibility criteria and administrative procedures that effectively restrict loan guarantees to firms where they will really make a difference. For example, set fees and premiums to reflect the true costs of providing the guarantee. This will help screen out both too healthy and too weak candidates. In addition, leave a sufficient percentage of the loan unguaranteed to provide an incentive to the private lender to screen and monitor effectively.

VI. Besides Directing Capital Flows Through Influencing Private Financial Intermediaries, A State Can Create Its Own Public Financial Intermediaries.

In employing this tool, the state either borrows in the capital market or taxes the wealth of its residents to raise funds for enterprises it believes do not have sufficient access to private financial institutions' capital.

■ In this field of development finance, the giants have feet of clay. State authorities which sell tax-exempt bonds to finance business enterprises raise amounts of capital far eclipsing any other kind of state financial intermediary. But this huge volume of financing obscures their general impotence and poor targeting. Industrial revenue bond financing is primarily a vehicle for subsidizing the cost of capital. Unfortunately, the reduced costs of production these subsidies provide to the beneficiary corporations do not amount to much in light of total production cost or market differences among states. And their effect is further neutralized by the fact that most states offer them. Besides their dubious benefits, IRBs have hidden costs for the issuing state.

■ Bond-financed state financial intermediaries can be transformed from ineffective subsidy programs into institutions that help make capital available to smaller firms suffering from financial market imperfections. However, just placing a ceiling on the amount of individual IRB issues, or on the size of eligible companies, will not accomplish this goal. Something more must be done. The key change would appear to be offering some collateral or security to the bond purchaser beyond the future income of the recipient firm. There are two methods of providing this security. One is to insure the bonds with state mortgage insurance, and the other is to actually back the bonds with the full faith and credit of the state.

■ An alternative to bond-financing of a public lending institution is tax-financing. On the one hand, intermediaries funded independently of the private capital market have greater freedom to abandon the undesirable behavior of conventional lenders; this allows them to better serve capital-starved small firms, for example. But this freedom can permit new kinds of inefficiency, as well as entailing other costs. Also, taking sizable amounts of tax revenue for these programs may be very difficult.

■ The vicissitudes of tax financing argue for primarily tax-financed state financial institutions seeking other compatable sources of funds. One possible source is state pension funds. Another is the federal government's economic development programs. Finally, there is the bond market. Having a tax-financed institution go to the bond market for part of its capital is not necessarily equivalent to setting up a bond-financed program from scratch.

■ Regardless of how they are financed, state intermediaries that provide only debt—loans with fixed, regular repayment terms—cannot satisfy all unmet small business capital needs. Any state that is serious about nurturing enterprises that have been unjustifiably refused funds from conventional sources must provide for equity financing as well. In contrast to debt, equity represents capital supplied to a firm in return for some share of its uncertain future income. This type of financing gives brand new businesses a critically necessary holiday from capital costs until they begin generating positive cash flows.

■ While development finance has historically been concerned with finding sources of capital for needed uses, states are also faced, in their capacity as investors of trust and operating balance funds, with finding the best uses for an already existing source of capital. Although constrained by both law and demands that they produce certain kinds of income flows, these funds can represent an important pool of development capital.

VII. States Can Respond To Many Housing And Infrastructure Financing Problems With The Same Kinds of Tools Used To Nurture Small Business Enterprise.

States have tried to stimulate housing and public works by changing administrative regulations, implementing capital subsidy and guarantee programs, and creating state housing financial intermediaries and municipal bond banks.

Capital market imperfections prevent many families from financing home ownership, even when they can pay the costs that an efficient market would demand of them. State governments can help solve the problem.

■ Anti-redlining codes can help ensure that home mortgage loan applicants are judged on their relevant individual credit characteristics, rather than inappropriate ones like age of the property or race. State regulators must, on the one hand, require lenders to go beyond typical prejudicial early stage screening criteria, but at the same time permit them to vary mortgage terms and interest rates in response to actual differences in risk producing characteristics. They must bring forth the information needed for determining who is redlining, and who is not. And they must provide a sanction powerful enough to outweigh any perceived benefits of improper discrimination. Finally, new state anti-redlining regulatory initiatives must be especially good in order to justify themselves, since a whole range of like-minded statutes already exist at the federal level.

■ Exceptionally high interest rates accompanying periods of high inflation this decade have made usury ceilings a serious barrier to the availability of mortgage credit. This situation particularly hurts the less favored mortgage applicant. Several states have gone to the heart of the problem and reformed their usury laws. The best solution is probably a floating usury ceiling, gauged to some index of competitive market interest rates.

■ Besides placing a ceiling on mortgage interest rates, most state governments have discouraged lenders from offering variable rate mortgages. This type of mortgage allows for adjustment of its interest rates as market interest rates change. The VRM can generally help increase the availability of mortgage loans by guaranteeing that the lending institution will be getting a high enough interest return from its mortgage assets to attract deposits by paying out a competitive interest rate.

■ A handful of state governments have attempted to influence the flow of private home mortgage funds through reducing the risks lenders must assume in making such loans. This is accomplished through home mortgage loan guarantee programs, which should be structured much like small business mortgage loan guarantee programs.

■ The obstacles to a successful bond-financed state home mortgage intermediary mirror those barriers to an effective bond-financed state business loan intermediary. Like their business financing relatives, state housing finance agencies primarily rely on revenue bonds to raise capital. Since they are secured only by the repayment of mortgage principal and interest, these bonds tend to be marketable only if investors believe they are being used to finance home buyers the private market would normally find bankable. Some state and local single family home mortgage programs have also become vehicles for interest subsidies targeted at middle income home buyers, in order to attract them back to the central city. But these subsidies have about as much impact on residential location as the industrial revenue bond-delivered subsidy has on business location.

As one of the least organized sectors of the American capital market, the sub-markets for local governmental debt stand ripe for intervention. Already several states have recognized and taken advantage of this opportunity for improving the capacity of their counties and cities to raise capital. They illustrate how state governments can make capital availability to localities more closely mirror those jurisdictions' ability to repay rather than reflecting breakdowns in financial intermediation.

■ The absence of federal regulation of state and local borrowing has left a large gap that continually creates problems for local government bond issues. In particular, the absence of registration and disclosure requirements has meant a dearth of trustworthy and easily acquirable information for prospective suppliers of funds. States can mandate standard accounting procedures for their local governments to help assure the availability of necessary credit information. They can also assume authority to approve or reject local bond sales on the basis of compliance with disclosure requirements.

■ An alternative approach would be to remove bond rating agencies and private investors from the risk assessing and bearing process for local government issues, substituting in a state government agency. This is done for some bond issues in a handful of states through municipal bond guarantee programs.

■ Even with a municipal bond guarantee, local governments still face many problems in dealing directly with the capital market. A part of the solution lies in state-owned municipal bond banks, which act as financial intermediaries for these borrowers. These institutions can reduce transaction costs, economize on information costs, and in some cases provide otherwise unavailable opportunities for risk diversification. They will make their greatest contribution in states where most localities are small in size.

VIII. *Capital-related Policies Can Be Used To Give Even More Concentrated Assistance To Depressed Communities In A State.*

Given the need to give a greater push to development in some places as opposed to others, how can a state government employ capital-related policies to help out?

Generally, the principles of development finance we have laid out in previous chapters can be applied to substate development problems with certain modifications. Most importantly, the caveats apply. Just as supplying capital statewide will not necessarily lead to more investment, more jobs and higher incomes, boosting the supply of capital in a depressed substate region will not necessarily rescue that area. The reason is the same: factors other than the cost and availability of capital typically determine the level of investment in any area. Nevertheless, there are opportunities for effective development finance in depressed areas.

■ While the unavailability of capital for viable enterprises does not account for the basic plight of depressed areas, these places do contain some opportunities for business, housing and infrastructure development possessing all the necessary ingredients for success except capital. A state can give priority to obtaining funds for these competitive but capital poor projects in these communities. In essence, it will be rationing market-perfecting intervention on the basis of need.

■ In addition, subsidies delivered through a below market cost of capital can be used to compensate enterprises for the added costs of operating in a depressed area. These firms may be already located in the area, or considering moving or starting up there. We have taken a guarded view of such capital subsidies when used to promote statewide economic development, and offer some of the same criticisms of their use in aiding substate regions. Nevertheless, it should be entertained as one tool in the development finance kit.

■ Saving endangered plants may sometimes be a cost-effective way of "creating" jobs. Plant closing sometimes represents essentially profitable operations that have not been managed properly. Under circumstances of this type, far from having to prop up a non-competitive business, a community simply needs to effect a transfer of ownership to people who can run the firm efficiently. In the other case, the plant may in fact not be profitable when compared to other investment opportunities of similar risk that the owners' have available to them. But the operation may be very far from being in the red. Such a plant may be able to continue at a profit that is acceptable to an employee or resident-employee ownership group.

■ Developing job opportunities in depressed areas will not, by itself, ensure that unemployed or low income people adequately benefit from them. This argues for targeting beyond geographical areas to specific types of individuals who are deemed most in need of assistance. Furthermore, whom a depressed area firm should hire is only one example of an important social cost or benefit which a state government may want to take account of in the development process. Jobs created through development are not all the same. For example, part of the employment generation by small firms involves inferior working conditions.

■ Once a decision has been made to encourage investment in depressed areas, having institutions at the state level placing all kinds of conditions on firms receiving capital may not be the most effective way for dealing with externalities and equity considerations. This may be more appropriately the role of local, community-based organizations. After all, the residents of the community in which a venture is located bear many of its external effects. To the extent a venture must answer to its community, it will also be responsive to these impacts in its decisions. State governments should offer more capital assistance for community-based development.

1
FACING REALITY

The initial attraction of capital markets for economic development planners is based on the obvious fact that without buildings, equipment and inventories—the means of production known as capital—economic activity would not take place. It goes without saying that capital formation is crucial to the process of economic growth. Increases in per capita income are largely dependent on growth in the productivity of each worker. In turn, the productivity of labor is largely a reflection of the quantity and quality of capital goods available to work with. It is important to understand from the outset, however, that although capital is a necessary ingredient in a profitable enterprise, it is insufficient in and of itself. Without a good market, good labor, good raw materials and good management, good financing will make no difference. Good money cannot make a bad deal good. Often, in fact, good money can conceal real flaws in markets, management or production until it's too late to repair the damage.

On the other hand, the wrong kind of money—debt instead of equity, for example, or short-term debt instead of long—can totally jeopardize an otherwise good deal, and the lack of capital can keep otherwise good enterprises from getting off the ground. For instance, a rapidly growing, highly profitable $50 million electronics firm in Massachusetts was recently told by its banker that the solution to its perennial money problems was to stop growing. That may have been good from the banker's point of view, but it is hardly salutary from an economic development standpoint. The firm got its new plant financed in Ireland and 300 new jobs were created there instead of in Boston. This is not an isolated example. Very rapid, job-creating growth creates just such an insatiable demand for more and more capital. Without more capital there is no more growth; without more growth there are no new jobs.

THE LIMITED ROLE OF CAPITAL

What then is the relationship between capital and state economic development? To begin with, the actual process of capital formation within a state is dependent on the decisions of private firms to do business there. In the course of initiating a new enterprise in a state, expanding an existing one, or relocating an old one, businesses demand various kinds of financing. The demand for capital, however, largely depends on factors other than capital supply.

It depends on whether the state represents an attractive place to invest, given its market conditions and other production costs.

These profound forces must first be understood before we can assess how increasing capital supply or reducing capital costs can help out firms, state or regions.

The Power of the Market Place

The real forces which determine whether or not a state is an attractive place to invest are the enormous interregional and international shifts taking place in populations, purchasing power, labor supply, energy and raw materials in real goods markets on a worldwide basis. The effects of these changes are now visible in declining regions such as the Midwest and Northeast, declining cities such as Akron and Trenton, and declining neighborhoods such as South Boston and East Los Angeles. These areas are competing in a world economy in which they are on the short end of both relatively declining markets (on the demand side) and relatively increasing costs and decreasing availability of such key factors of production as labor, land and raw materials (on the supply side).

The past 30 years have seen major changes in the distribution of population and employment. Since 1950, suburbs have grown faster than either central cities or rural areas. Until 1970, it was also true that metropolitan areas were growing faster than rural ones. Since 1970, however, this trend has reversed itself: rural places are now actually growing faster than metropolitan ones. Indeed, central cities as a group have actually lost population in absolute terms. Expressed in numbers, we see the following picture. From 1960 to 1970, non-metropolitan areas lost 3.2 million people, while metropolitan places gained 4.2 million people. But between 1970 and 1974, rural areas gained 1.5 million people, while the large metropolitan areas (those with over 1 million people) lost 1.7 million residents (Bureau of the Census, 1977; Birch, 1977).

Along with these shifts in population have come changes in the interregional and intra-metropolitan location of employment. There have been three types of movements: from industrial regions of the U.S. to less industrial regions, from metropolitan areas to rural areas within the same region, and from central cities to their suburbs. The South Atlantic, East South Central and Pacific regions have increased their shares of employment faster than their shares of population, while the Middle Atlantic and East North Central regions have had just the opposite experience. Nationwide, rural area employment has grown faster (or in some cases declined less) than metropolitan employment. Finally, within certain regions of the country, central cities have had absolute declines in employment between 1947 and 1972. This is especially true in the Northeast; in the South and West, even central cities have experienced substantial employment growth. But regardless of regional location, the central cities of large SMSAs have held a declining share of metropolitan jobs (Bureau of the Census, 1974; Chinitz, undated).

Behind the changing patterns of population and employment are basic decisions by households about where to live and work, business firms about where to invest, and governmental units about where and how to tax and spend.

People choose where to live and work for a variety of economic, social, physical and personal reasons: the quality of schools and neighborhoods, the availability of jobs and level of taxes, the climate and environmental quality, the proximity of friends and family, and many other reasons.

Business firms, in deciding where to invest, respond not only to shifts in the location of markets for their products, but also to changes in the cost and availability of the capital, labor and land they need for production.

There is some dispute among analysts as to whether people follow jobs or jobs follow people. In other words, has the growth in markets and labor supply due to independent population shifts been more important in determining business location than independent business location shifts in influencing people to move? Although the preponderance of research shows that the interregional movement of jobs and investments tends to follow the migratory patterns of people (Muth, 1968; Wheat, 1973; Steinnes, 1977), this is not uniformly true, and there is evidence to the contrary (Olvey, 1970; Greenwood, 1973).

The interplay of population shifts, market growth and job location can be seen in contemporary patterns of regional growth and decline.

Population shifts to rural areas and the Sunbelt have occurred for a variety of reasons (Morrill, 1978) which in large part reflect deeply embedded ideological values for newness and nature. Although these values have existed for a long time, it has only been more recently that certain conditions have enabled them to be expressed. Among these conditions are the extension of transportation systems allowing people to live in regions just beyond metropolitan areas, and the "metropolitanization of the countryside," whereby rural electrification, television, shopping centers and such have made certain "urban" amenities available in non-urban locations. Conversely, many metropolitan amenities have vanished with the growth of pollution, poverty and crime in the central city. Moreover, retirees, a group of people with a high preference for non-urban locations, have been growing in number as the population ages, retirement comes earlier, and retirement incomes grow. In the background, a reduction in the birthrate has eliminated a population growth factor that previously masked outmigration from metropolitan areas (Alonso, 1978).

These movements of people have to a large degree *led* job movements. The migration of households has created new market areas and enlarged labor pools in rural areas and outside the Northeast and Midwest (Vaughan, 1977). But beyond this population led change, an independent historical shift in the geographic structure of American industry has been at work. As economist Wilbur Thompson argues, manufacturing employment has traditionally filtered down through a national system of cities. In this system, new industries were born in the old manufacturing belt, and as they matured and became more routinized, they could afford to seek cheaper and often less skilled labor and land and raw materials outside the major manufacturing centers.

Now the birth stage itself has been shifting to places outside the old manufacturing centers (Sternlieb, 1975). Previously remote, small and medium-sized cities of the South and West have become more suitable as sites for starting up new industries and firms. There are two reasons for this. The trend of industrial technology has been to develop techniques which lower the skill level required to produce new products and processes, and thus de-emphasize the advantages of old, metropolitan centers. In addition, highway systems in non-metropolitan areas have knitted together clusters of smaller communities into good labor, business services and product markets. At the same time, the cities of the old manufacturing belt have become less attractive as places to incubate new industries. A major problem is that these regions have an infrastructure not well suited to many contemporary firms. For example, the assembly of land may be difficult due to the fact that it has already been so subdivided. The social dimension of this growing unattractiveness is the power of trade unions in the Northeast and Midwest, as well as the extensive social welfare system of those areas, which limits the flexibility of private capital.

The Relative Importance of Capital, Labor and Land

While proximity to growing markets for its products is the dominant consideration in location decisions for most firms, it is by no means the only factor. For example, a venture that exports its products nationwide or worldwide may care more about differences in production costs among various possible sites.

Only when such differences in production costs—as opposed to market proximity—become important factors in investment location can one even begin to talk about the role of capital. For capital, along with labor, land, energy and raw materials is a principal cost of production. Which one of these costs weighs most heavily in an investment location decision depends on a combination of two things, the proportion of total costs accounted for by the particular resource, and the degree to which those costs vary geographically.

Capital appears to strike out on both counts. Total annual capital costs (depreciation, interest and after-tax profits) are generally only about 10 percent of the total value of sales for a corporation (IRS, annual). And while data on interregional differences in the cost capital is limited, what we do know indicates that they are not substantial. One study shows, for example, that the rates for the average business loan typically differ between the North and South by less than three-quarters of one percent (Staszheim, 1969). A more recent study shows typical interregional differences in loan rates to be even less. In November 1977, the average rate of interest charged for long-term business loans was 7.4 percent in New York, 7.6 percent in the Southeast and 7.7 percent in the Southwest (Birch, 1977).

By contrast, labor is the major production cost in most industries. For each dollar of business income in the corporate sector, 83.3 cents goes to wages and salaries and only 13.8 cents for payments to capital owners (net interest and after-tax profits) (Bureau of Census, 1978). Moreover, unit labor costs vary geographically, a result of differences in productivity and wage rates. One researcher found that employment grew faster in regions with the highest ratio of value added to wages (Vaughan, 1977). According to the vice president of the Fantus Corporation, the leading plant relocation consulting firm, "Labor costs are the big thing far and away. Nine out of ten times you can hang industrial moves on labor costs and unionization."

The costs of other resources, such as land and energy, vary from place to place as well. For example, the South has significantly lower land prices and a slower rate of increase in those prices, whereas land prices in the Northeast and East North Central states are well above the U.S. average (Birch, 1977). For firms that are land intensive, location in one region as opposed to another can clearly have a significant effect on production costs.

The Powerful Impact of Federal Policy

State policy makers concerned with developing an economically sound development strategy have to contend not only with the whole thrust of powerful world economic forces, but with the fact that federal government intervention in those markets (through tax, expenditure and regulatory policy) is far more powerful than any tools available to the state.

In general, the federal government's huge half *trillion* dollar budget has one of two kinds of effects on economic development. It either affects the level and character of demand at different locations, or the cost and availability of human and material resources used by producers. It causes these effects by decision as to who gets taxed how much and where, who benefits from expenditures, or who is affected by regulation.

How federal policies shape the geography of economic growth in the United States has been catalogued in a recent major survey by the Rand Corporation (Vaughan, 1977). The most important of these policies and their effects, some of which are direct and intentional, and others which are indirect and unintended, are summarized here.

Federal policies that change the pattern of population migration and housing location have a powerful indirect impact on economic development. They influence both the market size and labor supply of regions. Policies of this kind (such as Federal Housing Authority (FHA) and Veterans Administration (VA) housing credit, highway construction, and low-priced energy) have favored migration from the central city to the suburb, large metropolitan areas to rural areas, and older regions to younger regions.

Direct federal expenditures have tended to favor states in the South versus the old manufacturing belt. The latter has historically received much lower per capita public works and defense expenditures.

Specific fiscal and monetary policies vary in their effects. The investment tax credit has worked to the advantage of suburbs, rural areas and younger regions, since new plant construction, whose cost is reduced by the credit, tends to occur in these regions. The same is true of rapid depreciation allowances which shorten the apparent life of depreciated assets below their real life. Both have the effect of accelerating the redistribution of employment away from historic manufacturing districts in central cities, metropolitan areas and older cities. In contrast, when the personal income tax rate is reduced, the old manufacturing belt benefits because of its still higher per capita money income.

Labor supply has been influenced in subtle and complex ways. Unemployment insurance and welfare have increased the cost and reduced the availability of unskilled labor in old established industrial areas, where such payments are relatively high. Federal labor law has fostered the growth of trade unions, whose relative vigor in the old manufacturing belt has put this area at a labor cost disadvantage relative to the less unionized South.

The most important federal impact on the interregional cost of production has resulted from the development of an interstate highway system. These highways have opened up areas of the country (for firms using truck transportation) which otherwise would not have been potential industrial sites, particularly in Mountain and Southern states.

Interregional transportation costs have been affected by regulatory policy as well. Federal regulation of rail freight rates has kept them artificially high, to the disadvantage of older rail-based cities. This has caused firms to locate or expand in areas served well by trucking and in sites closer to growing markets outside old central cities and metropolitan areas.

Energy availability in the Northeast has become a more serious problem than need be as a result of federal price regulation reducing the incentive for producers in the South and West to supply it outside their home states. At the same time, these policies have also kept the price of energy down for firms in the Northeast.

Profound world economic forces and federal actions constrain the ability of states to affect economic activity through policies of any kind, let alone capital market ones. The demand for capital, and the corresponding attractiveness of a state for investment, depends primarily on whether it has a growing market and on its supply of resources other than capital. Investment did not increase seven times faster in Southern states than in New England states between 1967 and 1978 because the South has more savings, or cheaper loans, or better banks (Hovey, 1979). In fact, much of the capital to finance that growth flowed in from the North. It is not the superior *supply* of capital in those states but a superior *demand* for it that has generated their more rapid investment growth.

But simply because capital does not lead the way does not mean that well-functioning capital markets are not a critical enabling factor in state economic development. On the contrary, opportunities for employment and income growth may go unrealized when capital markets fail to channel funds to enterprises that could use them most productively. Capital is a necessary but insufficient condition. Its presence usually cannot make up for lack of markets or management, labor or raw materials. But the absence of capital, when all other factors are in place, can keep a firm from generating new jobs and economic activity.

WHO GETS CAPITAL AND WHY

The central issue in thinking about financial markets and state economic development is whether capital is being made available to those enterprises that can employ it most productively. We can imagine the capital allocation process as one in which ventures competing for funds are assigned a place in a queue. Those coming first will have first claim on capital at the lowest price. The public policy question is: On what basis are the places in line assigned?

Those in line are waiting for a crack at the limited new pool of savings generated each year by U.S. households and businesses. In 1976, this "new pool" amounted to approximately $380 billion, with seven out of every ten dollars saved by households. These owners of savings are the ultimate suppliers of capital. One out of four of these household savers will choose to deal directly with those in the credit queue; that is, they will buy stocks or bonds in a company selling a public issue. Usually, however, this whole process occurs through a web of institutions and mechanisms known as *capital markets,* with agents acting for savers. These agents, collectively called *financial intermediaries,* are often banks or other thrift institutions, pension funds and insurance companies (The Conference Board, 1977).

For an enterprise to get a good place in the queue, it must convince these savers, or their intermediaries, that its use of funds will offer them the most return on their money. Enterprises "bid" against one another for a priority position by attempting to convince capital suppliers that the investment projects for which they seek funds will provide superior, or at least sufficient, return.

Savers and their intermediaries are not only interested in the probable return that an enterprise can offer. They are also concerned about risk. Risk arises because of uncertainty about the rate of return on an investment project. A venture whose rate of return is more variable will be more "risky"; that is, returns *may* be much lower than expected. Suppliers of capital view this risk negatively, and either demand a higher rate of return, or avoid the risk altogether. This means that for a higher risk enterprise to get a good place in the capital allocation queue, it must be able to offer a high rate of return. And the reverse holds true as well: Lower risk enterprises may move to the front even though they offer a relatively lower rate of return.

Based on the story so far, we have the following picture of our credit line. Standing at the very front are those seekers of capital who can present evidence of both relatively higher probable return and lower risk to those who control savings and thereby supply capital. Languishing at the end of the line are those enterprises that present both low return and high risk. Funds are likely to be exhausted before they make it to the window. All the rest line up in between, with those offering the highest return relative to risk coming first.

Does this process "make economic sense"? At first glance, it appears sound. Those enterprises that can offer savers the highest return relative to risk are those with the best investment projects, whether digital computers or leather tanning. Firms that would produce in too costly a fashion are discriminated against, as they should be. Ventures that produce unmarketable goods are at a disadvantage, as they should be. Firms that can produce the highest return relative to the risk borne by suppliers of capital receive an advantage, as they should.

Nevertheless, under close scrutiny, the capital allocation process proves to have a number of flaws. Its failures fall into two broad categories. One class of failure prevents the financing of investment projects that do in fact offer a competitive *private* return. This problem is relevant to state economic development because jobs and incomes that might be created—at virtually no cost to the public—are lying dormant. This type of capital market failure reflects several different imperfections in the financial system. First, ventures may be held further back in the queue than need be due to the failure of mechanisms that could minimize risk to potential capital suppliers. Second, the agents at the window (our financial intermediaries) may not have accurate or sufficient information about certain kinds of firms, putting these enterprises at a disadvantage in seeking funds. Third, the high transaction costs of making and following some loans may keep certain ventures out of the line altogether (or cause them to be denied service once they get there). Fourth, some financial intermediaries in a monopoly position may exercise market power, raising a barrier to funding a project higher than it would be under open competition. Fifth, savers or their intermediaries may be prejudiced for reasons of race, sex, or politics. And sixth, government regulation and intervention in capital markets may have unintended side effects that distort the order of the credit line.

The other class of capital market failures prevents the financing of investment projects that do not offer a competitive private return but provide compensating social benefits. No incentive exists for giving a better place in line to such enterprises. This problem is relevant to state economic development primarily because it means jobs and incomes will not necessarily be created for those communities most in need.

In order both to understand why capital is often not available to otherwise productive firms and to suggest legitimate strategies for state intervention in capital markets, it is essential to recognize these causes of capital market failure (Daniels and Kieschnick, 1978). Each is spelled out in detail below.

Inefficient Risk Bearing

Future returns flowing from current investment cannot be known with certainty in advance. There is always a risk that actual returns on capital investment may be less than expected. Individuals who supply capital and expect returns are subject to this risk, and will either demand compensation for bearing it in the form of a greater return (or risk premium), or they will not make the investment at all.

To see that risk is borne in the most efficient manner—that is, such that risk premiums demanded by investors are at a minimum so all reasonably profitable ventures are funded—certain capital market conditions must exist. In the ideal capital market, investors hold portfolios including fractional claims (shares of stock, bonds) on a large number of investment projects. By holding a portfolio, an investor can reduce variability of his overall return below the average variability of each component investment standing alone. This *risk pooling* stems from the fact that some of the variability reflects factors unique to a particular investment. In a portfolio, these "non-systematic" risks cancel each other out.

All risk cannot be diversified out of existence, however, because separate investment returns move together as the economy rises and falls. This risk is "systematic." The systematic variability that an investment project contributes to a portfolio represents the incremental risk investors must bear when they hold a share in it. The more sensitive an investment project is to national economic conditions, the greater is its contribution to systematic risk and the greater will be the return it must offer to compensate people who own it.

An enterprise's risk cannot be *pooled* unless it can be *spread* among a large number of investors so that its non-systematic risk can be cancelled out in each individual portfolio. This *risk spreading* can be accomplished through two capital market mechanisms. Either shares of its equity and debt can be held by a large number of investors who buy its stock and bonds. Or the investment can be financed by a single financial intermediary, whose portfolio can be thought of as a combined portfolio of all its depositors and owners which is so large that even a sizable share in the enterprise can be effectively risk pooled.

When a business is not financed through capital market mechanisms in which a large number of investors can own shares in it, or by financial institutions who can pool risk, then investors in the enterprise will not be able to diversify away all "non-systematic" risk. It will therefore either have to produce an inefficiently high return to compensate for this additional risk, or be denied capital altogether.

Excessive Transaction and Information Costs It takes time and professional resources to arrange a financial transaction. These transaction costs—the time of the entrepreneur, financier, lawyers and accountants to write a business plan, prepare financial statements, negotiate the deal, and complete the investment agreement—represent real business costs and do not themselves indicate a market failure. The higher the transaction and information costs, the higher the rate of return to justify funding an investment. The costs can in fact get so high that the result is not to fund the deal.

Much of the history of financial intermediaries in the United States has been the reduction of transaction and information costs. For example, auto loans, home mortgages and credit cards are so standardized and streamlined that the transaction and information costs for consumer lending are very low. And the published information and easy buying and selling of stocks makes those costs for large corporations almost zero.

These costs are still, however, a greater obstacle to many financial deals than they should be in well-functioning capital markets—

especially for smaller firms.

To begin with, to the extent that the investor is risk averse, he or she will demand both more information and a tighter investment agreement. In the words of one economist (Stigler, 1967), "information costs are the costs of transportation from ignorance to omniscience, and seldom can a trader afford to take the entire trip." The less risk averse the investor, the shorter the trip need be. Thus one way to reduce information and transactions costs is to reduce risk aversion by improving risk spreading or pooling. If the actual risk of any single investment is reduced by the pooling of many investments, the individual investor does not need as much information about any single investment.

Moreover, once information is obtained, it could then be provided at little or no cost to additional potential investors. Thus it should ideally be priced near zero. But the large initial costs of searching out information mean that in practice a private provider, say Moody's or Standard and Poor's, will either charge a price above this near zero incremental cost (thus reducing its availability) or will not provide the information at all. Consequently, the price of information to financial institutions may be too high to be worth having.

Finally, many of the transaction costs incurred in financial deals are imposed by public regulation. Many legal and accounting fees are paid to ensure compliance with these regulations. The intent is to reduce fraud, and thus ensure that securities are traded in more efficient markets whose investors can trust information. The burden of these transaction costs is uneven, however, and falls upon certain types of ventures—especially younger and smaller ones—making it too expensive for them to raise funds in major capital markets.

The consequence of these different ways in which information and transaction costs are inefficiently raised is to price many otherwise sound ventures out of the market. Or, if for some reason financial intermediaries do not think they can pass these costs on, the higher cost ventures will simply not be financed.

Lack of Competition Among Financial Institutions

Traditional economic theory suggests that in markets with one or few participants, producers tend to restrict supply in order to charge higher prices and gain higher profits. This situation occurs in capital markets as well. Given the variety of somewhat compartmentalized capital markets (banking, venture capital, commercial paper, public bond, private placement, new issues equity, etc.), it is possible for market concentration to affect any or all of them. Some of these markets are also geographically localized, creating further opportunities for market concentration. One out of four U.S. counties, for example, has no more than two commercial banks. These usually rural counties are highly concentrated in the South and Rocky Mountain states.

A growing body of evidence shows concentration in the banking industry has an adverse impact on the performance of these financial intermediaries (Heggestad, 1979; Talley, 1977). Absence of competition intensifies risk aversion, which in turn produces increased interest rates and causes ventures over a certain risk level to be defined funds at any price. Again, the problem is not just that a marked imperfection such as monopoly power may increase the cost of money; the more serious consequence is that the otherwise deserving firm will be denied access to capital at all. The bank without competition will be able to charge lower risk borrowers high rates, making it unnecessary to give any loans to the higher risk ventures.

Discrimination by Financial Institutions

Discrimination against racial minorities and innovative organizational forms (worker-owned enterprises, community development corporations, and consumer cooperatives) comes in a variety of forms, as does discrimination against women, and against certain locations such as inner city neighborhoods. Financial institutions have comparatively little experience with these kinds of borrowers. In some cases, discrimination is the way financial institutions respond to high information costs. In other cases, outright racial or class prejudice exists, as does political distrust of the goals and implications of new organizational forms.

Each of these forms of discrimination can be thought of as perverse consequences of the ultimate capital market reality—that money flows on the basis of personal confidence in the borrower.

For example, experience with a particular borrower allows a financial institution to gain information and establish personal confidence in the financial relationship. Even in the absence of all other problems, financial institutions will favor established customers over the unknown and unfamiliar.

When investors cannot get quick, inexpensive information on borrowers, they often resort to using generalized characteristics such as skin color or sex or location as a short form for credit screening. These characteristics will only be *partially* and *indirectly* (if at all) associated with creditworthiness, but reliance on them effectively screens out many who, upon careful examination with more complete information, would be fully creditworthy.

Distortions by Public Regulation and Tax Policies

Government regulation of capital markets is usually based on some perceived market failure which the regulation is intended to perfect. The way governments tax capital reflects the conflicting goal of wanting to have a progressive tax system and yet not wanting to have disincentives for investment. Whether they accomplish their intended goals or not, most regulations and taxes serve to increase private risk aversion, or to impose added information and transaction costs on risky enterprises.

Some regulations determine who will be permitted to function as a financial intermediary. These kinds of regulations are a good place to start in understanding how primary intentions may have unintended, and adverse, secondary side effects. For example, federal and state chartering of commercial banks is intended to keep out unsound institutions. But one of the major causes of market concentration is these government-imposed barriers to entry.

Other regulations govern what assets banks, savings and loan associations, life insurance companies, and pension funds may hold— that is, to whom and for what purpose they may supply funds. Many of these asset regulations are designed to control the risk level of a financial intermediary and thus protect the depositor or policy holder. While intended to ensure the security of liabilities, these well-intentioned regulations have the effect of cutting off funds completely to risky enterprises that may nevertheless have a very high rate of return.

Price regulations exist as well, setting maximum interest rates financial institutions may pay depositors or the rates they can charge borrowers. Price controls on deposits are intended to prevent price wars between financial institutions and to protect some institutions who are dedicated to important public purposes. But difficulties arise when the returns savers can obtain in unregulated markets (such as treasury bills, commercial paper and certificates of deposit) exceed the ceilings in regulated markets. Then money flows out to unregulated institutions, and regulated institutions (such as savings and loan associations) cannot meet their loan demands. This forces the regulated institutions to extend fewer loans, and to refuse renewal of existing ones.

Finally, some public regulations, such as Securities and Exchange Commission registration, require firms selling securities to provide certain information on the transaction. As we have noted, there is a trade-off between the market-perfecting effects of more information and the market-distorting effects of the costs of that information. On the one hand, these disclosure requirements protect the buyer by reducing the incidence of fraud and increasing the likelihood that the investment is financially sound. However, providing all this information is very expensive. It dramatically increases transaction costs for any issue. Because these costs are relatively constant, they weigh far more heavily on small firms. In fact, they can be so heavy that small firms cannot afford to sell securities at all.

The level and incidence of taxes and how they are targeted inevitably affect capital markets. For instance, the gap between the tax rate on capital gains and the tax rate on earned income is meant as an "incentive" to increase capital formation by rewarding risk-taking in investments. The incentive is poorly targeted, however, as a large portion of the tax expenditure supports capital gains in land and timber ownership rather than in productive capacity.

Failure to Recognize Social Benefits or Equity Considerations Many of the effects of capital allocation may be completely external to the parties—suppliers and users of funds—involved in a market transaction. For example, when an enterprise leaves a city it may impose costs on the public—increased outmigration of other firms, rising unemployment and crime, etc.—far in excess of the costs that actually fall upon the particular firm. When an enterprise builds a plant introducing waste into the air and water, it may pay nothing for its "use" of that air and water, yet serious environmental costs are incurred. These external considerations, and countless others, tend to be ignored in the private allocation of capital.

Just as capital markets systematically fail to reward enterprises that produce certain social benefits or punish those that create public costs, they do not consider the equitable effects of who gets funds for investment. That an investment project is to be undertaken in an underdeveloped area, or by a cooperative or worker-owned enterprise, or by an individual from an historically marginal social class or group counts for nothing when places in the capital allocation queue are assigned.

THE SIGNIFICANCE OF CAPITAL MARKET FAILURE Are capital market imperfections that deny funds to otherwise profitable firms worth worrying about? At least two facts justify the concern of a state government. First, small enterprises are the overwhelming casualties of these imperfections. Second, firms of that size contribute crucially to job creation.

Recent research by David Birch at the Massachusetts Institute of Technology strongly contradicts the popular wisdom about how and why aggregate employment levels change over time (Birch, 1979). According to Birch:

■ All parts of the country—urban and rural, metro and non-metro, Sunbelt and Frostbelt—are losing jobs through the death and contraction of business establishments at just about the same rate: 8 percent per year. What makes the crucial difference between a declining area and a growing one is the rate at which these "lost" jobs are *replaced* with new ones through the birth of new establishments and the expansion of existing ones.

■ 66 percent of the "replacement" jobs are created by enterprises employing fewer than 20 people. More than 50 percent are generated by small independent firms. *Fully 80 percent are created by establishments under four years of age.* Relatively few "replacement" jobs are created by middle-sized or large firms.

■ The widely held view that *Fortune 500* firms "make all the difference" is, at best, only half true. For while branch plants and subsidiaries do create a significant amount of employment, the birth and expansion of independent single plant firms is equally important to job generation.

Consistent with these figures on the job creation power of small firms is evidence of their profitability. From 1958 to 1976, Federal Trade Commission figures show that manufacturing firms with less than $1 *million* in assets were—as a class of firms—just as profitable as those firms with more than $1 *billion* in assets. Indeed, in the last five years, small firms have substantially out-performed large ones. For example, between 1972 and 1976, U.S. manufacturing corporations with assets under $1 million produced an average after-tax return on equity of 15.95 percent, while firms with more than $1 billion in assets returned only 12.91 percent. It is important to note that these Federal Trade Commission figures *include failures* (Daniels and Kieschnick, 1978). Although it is true that the risk of these small firms as a class is somewhat greater than for large ones, their superior returns appear to offer a premium which warrants investors bearing that risk.

Are capital market failures that deny funds to enterprises that do not offer a competitive private return but provide compensating social benefits or distributional effects worth worrying about? As we will explain in Chapter 8, there is nothing in the "natural process" of state economic development that guarantees newly created jobs and incomes will go to the distressed parts of a state, that disadvantaged workers will be hired, or that new jobs will be "good jobs." Yet these outcomes are all important objectives for a development policy.

SUMMARY

Reality has hit home, calling into question some of our favorite (and stubborn) assumptions about the role of capital in state economic development. Capital is usually *not* the most significant missing ingredient in the development process. Depending on the kind of business, its age and location, the crucial impediment may be markets, or management, or the relative cost and availability of labor or land, or raw materials. Substantial population shifts from central cities to suburbs, from large metropolitan areas to former rural areas, and from older regions to younger ones, have had a vast impact on the two most important determinants of business location: expanding markets and available labor. Moreover, factors that made the old manufacturing belt an ideal place to incubate new industries no longer hold. Federal policy has encouraged these economic forces rather than counteracted them.

So the question becomes: If the *cost of capital* is relatively small in the overall costs of doing business, and the *availability of capital* is a necessary but insufficient factor in creating a profitable, growing job and tax producing enterprise, what other weapons does a state have in its arsenal to affect larger market and federal forces? What else can states do to influence the growth of markets and increase the availability of the essential factors of production? How can the state identify those kinds of enterprises and industries which can take particular advantage of the state's market position and its particular combination of human and physical resources? Chapter 2 looks at the impact of state tax, expenditure and regulatory policy on these market and production factors as they affect the creation and expansion of all sizes of businesses, but especially those larger firms for whom access to capital is not an issue.

Given this larger set of tools and policies, we can then turn to the specific issue of the state's potential influence on one factor of production—capital. Capital market failures may mean specific enterprises cannot get the funds they need, even though either private or social returns justify it. Sometimes this failure manifests itself in a firm having to pay an unnecessarily high and unachievable return to attract capital. Other times it shows up in a complete rationing away of credit at any price. In either case, capital is effectively unavailable.

In Chapter 3, then, we will begin to look more particularly at how the capital market imperfections we outlined here do in fact cut off access to capital for those young, small, profitable firms who produce half of our society's new jobs. Here, at last, access to capital, and the state's ability to influence that access, becomes of real importance.

2
STATE POLICIES AND ECONOMIC DEVELOPMENT

At best state economic development planners may be able to moderately influence the world economic and federal governmental forces described in the previous chapter. If they can influence these forces at all, it will be through a combination of long-term taxation, expenditure and regulation policies, of which capital market policies will be a single component.

Thus it behooves anyone interested in capital market policies to consider the larger picture of state government's influence on economic development. Its impact on private investment decisions occurs through three channels: the level and structure of state taxes; the level, location and composition of state expenditures; and the nature of state regulations.

In analyzing these three areas of potential state economic development policy, it is clear that many of the policies the states currently pursue are simply wrongheaded: Lowering business taxes and providing tax incentives, it turns out, makes virtually no difference in business location decisions, yet the states consistently compete with each other to give away scarce taxpayer dollars. On the other hand a coherent state expenditure and regulatory policy can make the whole state a far more attractive place in which to invest or build, and can have a profound influence on where economic activity takes place within the state. Few states appear to have thought through such policies.

This inattention is particularly unfortunate, for it is only through such policies that a state can influence the branch plant expansion decisions of larger firms, for whom capital availability is no problem at all. So although overall state tax, expenditure and regulatory policies affect all firms, these policies are the *only* way to affect large firms.

TAX POLICY Businesses have an almost obsessive regard (which they have effectively communicated to most state policy makers) for the impact taxes have on the profitability of doing business in a particular state. Yet, as we shall see, reality again contradicts the popular mythology. Three forms of taxation affect business operations directly or indirectly: taxes on business income and property, taxes on sales of goods and services, and taxes on personal income and property (Maxwell and Aronson,

1977). In evaluating the relative consequences of these three different taxes on state economic development, it is important to think of the state and local tax structure as *one* system, for that is how businesses regard it.

■ *Taxes on business income and business property.* Forty-five states have a corporate income tax, accounting for 5.6 percent of total state and local tax collections. In addition, as of 1973, all fifty states had some form of business property taxation, although this tax was becoming more important to local government units than to state governments. It accounted for 13.8 percent of state and local tax revenues in 1977.

■ *Taxes on sales of goods and services.* By 1973, forty-five states had a general sales tax and gross receipts which, in 1977, accounted for 24.6 percent of all state and local tax collections. Furthermore, selective excise taxes raised 9.9 percent of all revenues.

■ *Taxes on personal income and personal property.* As of January 1973, forty states had a personal income tax which, by 1977, accounted for 16.2 percent of all state and local revenues. Personal property taxes made up 21.8 percent of collections. (All figures from ACIR, 1979.)

Taxes on business income, property and inventories have the most visibility for those contemplating investment in a state and are frequently portrayed by firms and business organizations as being a serious deterrent to new investment. Yet, in fact, these business taxes typically account for only a very *small* proportion of total production costs. The Federal Reserve Bank of Boston has estimated that the average U.S. business pays 4.4 percent of its income to state and local government (in 1973, this meant .9 percent for corporate income taxes, 1.9 percent for property taxes, .8 percent for unemployment compensation contributions, and .8 percent for other business taxes) (Harrison and Kanter, 1978). To put this in perspective, in 1972, businesses paid approximately $1 in total state and local business taxes for every $20 paid out in wages and salaries. A mere 2 percent difference in unit labor costs among states could offset as much as a 40 percent difference in taxes among states (Cornia, et al., 1978). The relative importance of labor costs trivializes businesses' preoccupation with state and local business tax levels.

Even this minimal tax burden is neutralized by the federal corporate tax deduction for state and local taxes. In essence, this means the federal government ends up paying about one-third of a company's state and local tax bill.

Moreover, there has been substantial debate over who ultimately pays these remaining business taxes. For both corporate income and property taxes, it is difficult to come to any general conclusion about tax incidence. Who ultimately pays depends on the degree of competition prevailing in specific markets, on the sensitivity of a firm's supply and demand to price changes, on where the product is sold, and a host of other factors. Business taxes are often successfully passed on to consumers, further reducing the effective burden to those firms on which they were originally levied.

Finally, tax differentials are partially capitalized in land values. Land in a high-tax jurisdiction will have a lower price because of its tax liability. Conversely, land in a low-tax jurisdiction will have a higher price.

Given these facts, it should not be surprising that impartial research consistently concludes that there is little or no corresponding relationship between state and regional variations in business taxation and variations in economic growth (Thompson and Mattila, 1959; ACIR, 1963; Schmenner, 1978; Vaughan, 1979).

If state and local business taxes are generally unimportant to interstate business location decisions, it follows that tax incentives which reduce business taxes to influence business location are simply foolish. Tax incentives, like their close cousin, interest subsidies, are a waste of taxpayers' dollars. (We will spell out these issues more fully in Chapters 4 and 5.)

On the other hand, tax differences along border areas, and *within* states or particular metropolitan areas *may* influence investment location decisions, once the choice of a site has been narrowed to that point. Business location decisions are often a two-stage process—first a region is selected, and then a site within the region. Since prices of labor, materials and energy tend to be more uniform throughout a metropolitan area (and sometimes throughout a state) than across the nation as a whole, communities with lower local taxes may be able to attract investment away from local competitors. Research attempting to test this hypothesis has produced mixed results (Levin, 1974; Orr, 1975).

In turning from business and property taxes to sales and personal income taxes, a somewhat different set of issues arises, and conclusions are even more difficult to draw (Hyman, 1973). Both state sales taxes and personal income taxes have an impact on market demand conditions facing prospective investors. A retail sales tax is usually shifted forward 100 percent to the consumer. The total amount of income available for private expenditures in the state will be reduced, and sellers of privately purchased goods may as a whole suffer from reduction in total demand. State personal income taxes have a similar effect on demand.

Personal taxes affect state economic development in even more subtle but powerful ways. There is evidence that they influence population migration, changing both market size and labor supply

(Vaughan, 1978). In addition, personal taxes raise the cost of living, and workers who can will bargain for correspondingly higher wages (Izraeli, 1973). Since labor is generally the largest component of production costs, then *the most important impact of state and local taxation may be on relative labor costs.*

As with business taxes, the impact of personal tax differences within a metropolitan area is probably greater than that of personal tax differences between states. Some of the movement of affluent households to the suburbs has been an attempt to minimize taxes they would have to pay (through property, sales and income taxes) for social welfare in the central city (Aaronson and Schwartz, 1973; Bradford and Kelejian, 1973).

In general, the best available evidence suggests that the real effect of state taxes on investment location is grossly exaggerated. Taxes on businesses at prevailing levels make little difference, as we have seen. If any tax actually affects the fate of a business, it is probably the level of personal taxation. A relatively high level of personal taxation can negatively affect markets if it causes people to leave the state; it can negatively affect the cost of doing business if higher personal taxes are reflected in higher wage rates. (In an interesting confirmation of this reality, the Massachusetts High Technology Council—a private business interest group comprised of leading industrialists—recently struck a "social contract" with the state to expand employment dramatically in the state *not* in exchange for reduced business taxes, *nor* for more tax incentives, but rather for holding state and local personal taxes constant as a percentage of gross state product.) High levels of personal taxation may also affect the decisions of individual entrepreneurs to leave a state, taking their entrepreneurial energy and capital with them.

Perhaps the most dramatic impact results from any tax differentials between cities *within* a state. To the extent that such differences exist, they may adversely affect older and poorer communities by reducing the market and increasing the costs for those businesses that remain.

All of this analysis is not meant to suggest that state taxes can rise without bound and still not affect investment location decisions. Rather, the conclusions are based on prevailing levels of state taxation.

EXPENDITURE POLICY

How, where and how much a state chooses to spend will have a significant influence on *whether* it is an attractive place to invest and, perhaps even more significantly, *where* within the state development takes place.

Although state spending directly creates jobs—accounting for 4 percent of employment nationwide—this obvious impact obscures the more subtle but powerful effects. State expenditure produces goods and services that change the costs of production and the growth of markets for business firms. The development impact of state spending can be seen by examining the major categories of expenditure.

The largest single state expenditure is education, which commands approximately 50 percent of the combined state-local budget (Maxwell and Aronson, 1977). The quality of education in a particular state may affect a firm's ability to attract and maintain a qualified labor force. Since training workers adds to the cost of production, a state or sub-region that produces educated, skilled labor has an advantage over others. In fact, it has a double advantage, because high quality education can also cause more highly educated and skilled adult workers to migrate to the state or community, thereby enriching the labor pool.

Some evidence exists to support the argument that the quality of education influences the productivity of an area's labor force, and that this in turn affects the locational preferences of industry. In six of the fourteen industries analyzed by one researcher, the education of the labor force had a statistically significant impact on productivity (Sviekauskas, 1975). And evidence from a number of sources shows that at least for industrial location decisions within a metropolitan area, the quality of the labor pool matters greatly (Kemper, 1974; Stone, 1974; Steinnes, 1977). Specifically, firms relying on skilled workers have moved to the suburbs, where better-educated workers have already moved and where the level of educational attainment is generally higher (Vaughan, 1977). This evidence merely hints at the role state educational expenditure can play in economic development. It has not been verified empirically that interstate differences in average expenditure per pupil shape the quality of respective state labor pools in a significant way, or that these labor quality differences have an impact on interstate patterns of investment.

The second largest category of state expenditure is highway construction and maintenance—accounting for nearly 13 percent of state and local budgets (Maxwell and Aronson, 1977). Since transportation costs partially determine the markets a firm can reach and the prices it must pay for the resources it uses, such highway expenditures may influence the location choices of certain firms.

States have constructed highway systems primarily to link major cities. Such construction has simultaneously opened up new areas for industrial and residential expansion on the fringes of these cities. When such development created congestion on newly built intercity roads, beltways were constructed to circle and bypass the metropolitan areas. This created even more new land with access to truck and car transportation—either for shipping out products or for receiving commuting labor and other inputs.

Congested, rail-oriented inner cities have clearly been put at a disadvantage relative to newer, truck-oriented metropolitan areas. This is true regardless of whether the latter are in the suburban radius of a Frostbelt central city or a community in the Sunbelt. To the extent that rail-oriented cities are concentrated in particular states or regions, the decline of these regions has been accelerated by post-World War II state expenditure on intercity highways. At the very least, state provision of roads (in partnership with the federal government's Highway Trust Fund) enables plants to locate in places whose attractive energy, land and labor costs would otherwise be for naught.

The remaining balance of the state budget is split among a host of functional categories, including fire protection, recreation, public welfare and administration. These expenditures, most of which are for public services, in part can be described as *amenities*. Amenities include the availability of recreational and cultural facilities, the healthfulness of the environment, and freedom from fear of crime. Many of these may directly or indirectly reduce business operating and capital costs, and attract scarce senior technicians and professionals.

Survey research shows that firms are aware of, and to some degree sensitive to, public services when choosing a location. In Hartnett's study (1972), services ranked 13 out of 23 factors cited as "vitally important" by managers involved in relocation decisions. In a 1971 Economic Development Administration survey, police and fire protection were the two community expenditures most often singled out as primary.

The greatest impact of amenities on industrial location is probably a roundabout one, through their effect on the migration of households from state to state and community to community. If the attractiveness of a community stimulates migration, the labor pool will be deeper and markets will grow more rapidly (ACIR, 1967). One analysis has shown that cleaning up the air in Chicago to meet federal standards would produce average annual benefits worth $300 per household, with half this change reflected in lower wages necessary to attract labor to the area (Cohen, et al., 1974; Izraeli, 1973).

On balance, state expenditure policy is a good deal more significant as an economic development tool than state tax policy. Yet with a few recent exceptions, it has received little attention from state economic development policy makers (Daniels and Pfifferling, 1978). Thus the current influence of state expenditure policy may be unintentional, but it is nevertheless not neutral.

REGULATORY POLICY

State governments exercise a host of regulatory powers. Some affect the location of markets. Others affect the cost and availability of key factors of production including capital. We will hold the discussion of state regulation of capital markets for in-depth analysis in Chapters 4 ad 5 and concentrate here on those regulations which affect markets and other production costs.

Many state regulations influence the urban/rural distribution of population in a state (Hovey, 1977). These range from general land-use regulations that affect the location of highways, housing subdivisions, schools, hospitals, and shopping centers, to specific regulatory powers over sewage and water supply. Each of these powers directly or indirectly influences where population, and thus markets, grows or declines.

Regulations that affect population location also affect labor supply. And transportation regulations influence the cost of receiving raw materials and shipping finished goods to market.

State energy and environmental regulations influence both the cost and availability of alternative forms of energy and water quality processes. States, for instance, can impose (or relax) air pollution standards above those mandated by the federal government.

For businesses of any size, the cost in time and money of simply meeting regulatory red tape and paper work can be expensive. The weight tends to be proportionately heavier on smaller businesses. Some state such as Oregon and Washington have, however, sought to lessen this expense through "one stop" permitting. Instead of dozens of regulatory windows to visit, there is only one.

Rapidly expanding younger firms are often constrained, especially in older areas, by an enormous array of problems concerning labor supply, adequate land for expansion, adequate sewerage, water and infrastructure (Schmenner, 1978). Yet, to the best of our knowledge, with the exception of the (substate) North Carolina Research Triangle, no state provides the integrated approach to the provision of all these resources on a "turn-key" basis as does the Irish Development Authority (Daniels, 1978). When the Irish Development Authority convinces a firm to build a new plant in Ireland, they turn-key the entire operation: They see that access roads are built, sewer and water and energy lines are laid, a plant is found or built to specifications, and workers are recruited and trained. The response of firms to the thoroughness and professionalism of the IDA has been uniformly positive. Moreover, the IDA is careful to seek out only those rapidly growing firms whose market and production needs mesh well with Ireland's resources. The IDA provides a dramatic model for states to emulate, and represents a radical departure from the ineffectual boosterism that characterizes most state commerce departments.

Few states have defined these regulatory powers as an essential and relatively powerful factor in an intentional and integrated overall state economic development plan. This is unfortunate, for the exercise of these regulatory powers, particularly in conjunction with expenditure decisions, can have a significant economic development impact, particularly on the intrastate distribution of economic activity.

SUMMARY

Many state policies thought to promote economic growth do not work—they just cost taxpayers money. The preponderance of the evidence is clear: state taxes represent a small part of the cost of business; state tax incentives and subsidies generally do not change business decisions. If any state tax makes a difference, it is probably the effect of personal tax levels on markets and labor costs within and among states, and the differential impact of combined state and local taxes on business location decisions within the state.

Judicious use of state expenditure and regulatory policy can probably affect location decisions *within* the state, if they are carried out as a part of an integrated, systematic, long-term state economic development policy. And in exceptional circumstances, where a state neglects education, infrastructure or amenities over a long period of time, it makes the *entire state* less attractive to business. Finally, in a positive fashion, an aggressive state development agency like the Irish Development Authority could be a powerful force in attracting plant expansion to the state for those large firms who do not need capital.

We stress the word "judicious" in the above paragraph. Influencing economic development is not the only, or necessarily the primary, goal of state expenditure and regulatory policy. There are other dimensions of well-being in a state besides its rate of job and per capita income growth. For example, shifting expenditures from education for handicapped students to general vocational training programs may improve the quality of the state's labor pool, yet still be very undesirable. Or, relaxing land-use regulations may reduce barriers to development in an area, but destroy the quality of life for those already living there.

Finally, state expenditure and regulatory policies are only likely to be effective in aiding development if they take careful account of the far more pervasive world market demand and supply forces and the particular impact of federal policies on the state's economy. Within these constraints of markets and cost and availability of skilled people, land, energy, transportation and materials, *any* state government can determine those key industries for which the state has a real comparative economic advantage. These then can be encouraged by a discreet, focused, well-organized state economic development policy.

Massachusetts, for instance, has identified clear comparative economic advantages in the areas of high-technology development and financial services which are able to overcome the high costs of doing business and a declining local market by selling to a worldwide market. The state's mini-computer industry is so high-value added (and thus so able to overcome very high costs of production) that half of its product is "airmailed" out of Logan International Airport to Europe and Japan each evening. A more or less coherent state policy has been emerging over several administrations which seeks to incorporate tax, expenditure, regulatory and capital formation policy to support the birth and expansion of firms in these sectors (Daniels, 1977).

Alaska, in a radically different context, with very small population, great distance from markets, and the highest costs of production in the world, is recognizing a unique opportunity to develop its bottomfish industry into a world export market. One-fifth of the world's fish supply is in the Gulf of Alaska. A more or less coherent state policy is seeking to build infrastructure, develop markets and finance the construction and sale of harvesting and processing vessels and plants. In both cases each state enhanced a unique comparative economic advantage which recognized world market forces. Each state developed a relatively coordinated state policy which used tax, expenditure and regulatory strategies to enhance that market position. In both cases each state developed a strategy for appropriate intervention in capital markets, but only as a subsidiary part of a larger state effort.

Over time, states can actually change their comparative economic advantage through concerted state policy efforts. North Carolina has built up a formidable "research and demonstration" capability by providing strong support to its universities, by creating an attractive environment for professional people, and by developing coherent land use policy in the Research Triangle. The result is an internationally attractive industrial location which was just an idea twenty-five years ago.

It is only within the context of a well-thought-out and well-integrated economic development policy—which uses a full range of regulatory, expenditure and tax powers to focus on the state's particular economic and social strengths—that state planners can begin to think about those limited uses of state intervention in capital markets which can in fact stimulate new economic activity. That is the work we will now turn to in Chapter 3.

3
THE CAPITAL AVAILABILITY PROBLEM

It should now be clear that the role of capital in state economic development is limited. For firms of any size, markets and other key factors of production must first be in place. States affect all of these factors through the tax, expenditure and regulatory policies we have just reviewed.

When capital does enter the picture, its *cost* is seldom a major determinant in any business location decision. So state tax incentives or interest subsidies which offer to lower capital costs will seldom change a location decision.

The real capital issue is not the cost of capital but its *availability* to otherwise viable, growing firms, particularly those small young firms which create more than half of the net new jobs generated by our economy. It is precisely these small firms that are most likely to have difficulty gaining access to capital because of imperfections in capital markets. These are the firms which suffer from inadequate mechanisms for spreading and pooling risk, high information and transaction costs, various forms of prejudice, market concentration and the perverse consequences of federal and state government intervention in capital markets.

It is one thing to understand these issues in principle, and quite another to understand them in practical, work-a-day terms. Before we can begin to propose how states *ought* to intervene in capital markets to increase the flow of funds to these young, growing small firms, we must first understand *how* financial institutions operate in the capital marketplace, and how capital market imperfections deny appropriate kinds of capital in appropriate amounts at an appropriate price to these firms. We must also look at capital market imperfections that may impede the development of supportive housing and infrastructure.

EFFECT OF CAPITAL MARKET IMPERFECTIONS ON KEY SOURCES OF EMPLOYMENT GROWTH

As the following chart illustrates, an enterprise must be able to tap different sources and kinds of funds at different times over its life-cycle of growth. Foreclosing any one of them—particularly at its "stage" specific time of need—can have the same effect as depriving a

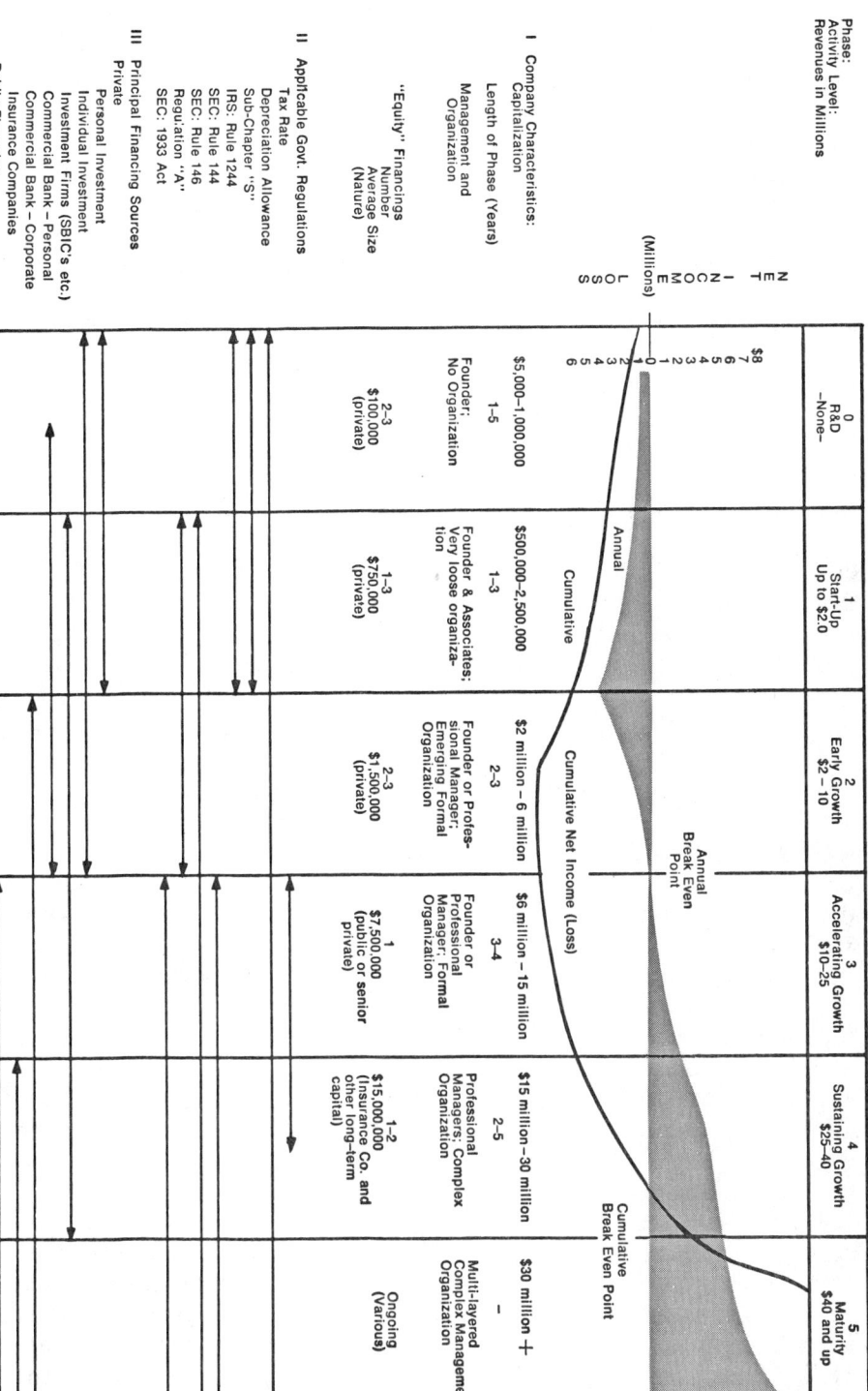

**Life Cycle of a New Enterprise
Model of a Growing and Successful Company**
1975-1976 Financial Market Conditions

Source: *Report of the SBA Task Force on Venture and Equity Capital for Small Business*, U. S. Small Business Administration, January, 1977.

developing organism of a vital nutrient. For example, during its first years a small firm will not be generating any positive net income, but will still need a constant inflow of funds for research and planning, acquisition of physical plant and equipment, and operating expenses. Financing here must largely be in equity form—that is, capital in exchange for a pro rata share in the firm's future income—rather than debt requiring periodic, regular payment of fixed interest and principal. Equity will not impose immediate demands for repayment; it is "patient" money. Moreover, debt financing will be difficult to acquire since the new venture has little collateral and no operating history. Once the enterprise begins production and marketing, it can rely somewhat more heavily on debt, if the repayment is spread out over a sufficiently long period of time and its ratio to a cushion of equity or ownership capital is reasonable. As it becomes more established, growth will accelerate, demanding rounds of equity financing along with heavier borrowing of long-term debt for expansion.

The crucial question here is how well different capital markets fulfill these needs for external equity and debt funds generated by small and young enterprises. Time and again, these firms are unable to obtain financing even though their rates of return (after an adjustment for risk) exceed the cost of capital, or (less typically) are charged a higher price for funds than would prevail in a fully competitive, efficient capital market.

To be perceived and treated as a small firm by the financial system, a company does not have to be a "mom-and-pop" store. The Small Business Administration, for example, permits Small Business Investment Corporation (SBIC) financing of firms if their assets do not exceed $9 million, if their net worth is not more than $4 million, and if their average net income after taxes is not more than $400,000. But in many segments of the capital market, a firm may have $50-100 million in assets and still be considered small (National Association of Securities Dealers, 1979).

Public versus Private Capital Markets   Those capital markets in which new, small enterprises suffer most are the *public* ones. These markets are called public not only because of any association they have with government, but because of two important "public" characteristics. First, the securities traded in them are standard and homogeneous, and therefore easily traded. Second, there is wide dissemination of relatively inexpensive information on companies trying to sell their securities in these markets. Public markets include the New York Stock Exchange, the American Stock Exchange, the over-the-counter market and various regional exchanges where equity shares are sold, as well as the national markets for corporate and municipal bonds.

In contrast to these public capital markets, within *private* capital markets contractual terms vary and information is harder to obtain, requiring negotiation between the supplier and demander of funds over the terms of investment. Private markets include commercial bank loans and the direct placement of corporate debt notes with insurance companies, pension funds and other financial institutions.

There are several advantages for the new or growing enterprise in being able to tap public as well as private markets. Both individual savers and financial intermediaries participate in the public markets. The volume of funds flowing through them is accordingly higher. For example, in 1977, $26 billion in corporate bonds were sold in public markets versus $15 billion in private ones (White and Light, 1979). Moreover, the large number of suppliers of funds seeking to buy securities in these markets makes for a relatively competitive atmosphere in which firms can obtain funds on the best possible terms. Since securities sold initially in a public market are reasonably uniform and well documented, they can also be easily resold in secondary markets, where investors trade securities that have been previously issued. This provides a liquidity of investment not obtainable in private markets where securities cannot be easily resold, and where firms must consequently pay a premium to suppliers of capital who hold illiquid (or not easily sold) investments.

Public Markets

Suppose a new or young, growing business in your state wants to seek funds in a public capital market. If the firm wants debt financing, this means selling corporate bonds. If equity financing is desired, then shares of stock in the company must be sold. To do either, the enterprise must first conform to certain public regulations concerning the issuing of securities and then enlist the appropriate financial advisors and institutions to help in selling its bonds or stock. This costs a substantial amount of money. During the 1930s the federal government established an elaborate regulatory structure—enforced by the Securities and Exchange Commission—to protect investors against fraud. One dimension of this is the requirement of legal registration, and accompanying disclosure of information, for any new publicly issued security. Administrative costs in preparing a statement of registration under the Securities Act of 1933 may run from $50,000 to over $100,000; the registration statement includes information on the proposed financing and the firm's history, existing business and future plans. The firm must then pay an underwriting business, or an investment banker, to act as middleman to sell the securities to investors. These costs of providing information and negotiating the transaction are largely fixed; they do not vary much with the size of the issue. This means that the cost of raising a dollar in funds for a smaller and younger company—whose total debt or equity issue will be relatively small—is greater than for a larger and more mature company making a more sizable issue. The following two tables illustrate the disproportionate costs in selling smaller issues of stock or bonds.

Table 1
Costs of Flotation as a Percentage of Proceeds for Common Stock Issues Registered Under the Securities Act of 1933 During 1971-1975; The Issues are Subdivided by Size of Issue and Method of Financing; Underwritten Cash Offers; Rights with Standby Underwriting; Non-Underwritten Rights

Size of Issue ($ millions)	Number	Compensation as a Percent of Proceeds	Other Expenses as Percent of Proceeds	Total Cost as a Percent of Proceeds
Underwritten Cash Offers				
Under .50	0	—	—	—
.50 to .99	6	6.96	6.78	13.74
1.00 to 1.99	18	10.40	4.39	15.29
2.00 to 4.99	61	5.59	2.87	9.47
5.00 to 9.99	66	5.50	1.53	7.03
10.00 to 19.99	91	4.84	0.71	5.55
20.00 to 49.99	156	4.30	0.37	4.67
50.00 to 99.99	70	3.97	0.21	4.18
100.00 to 500.00	16	3.81	0.14	3.95
TOTAL/AVG	484	8.02	1.15	9.17

NOTE: Issues are included only if the company's stock was listed on the NYSE, AMEX, or regional exchanges prior to the offering, any associated secondary distribution represents less than ten percent of the total proceeds of the issue, and the offering contains no other types of securities. The costs reported are (1) compensation received by investment bankers for underwriting services rendered, (2) legal fees, (3) accounting fees, (4) engineering fees, (5) trustees' fees, (6) listing fees, (7) printing and engraving expenses, (8) Securities and Exchange Commission registration fees, (9) Federal Revenue Stamps, and (10) state taxes.

SOURCE: Smith (1977).

Table 2
**Costs of Sale as a Percent of Proceeds—
Bonds, Notes and Debentures
1951-1955**

Size of Issue (in millions)	Compensation Costs	Other Costs	Total
Under 0.5	7.53	3.96	11.49
0.5 - 0.9	5.80	2.37	8.17
1.0 - 1.9	2.37	1.41	3.78
2.0 - 4.9	1.01	0.82	1.83
5.0 - 9.9	0.88	0.64	1.52
10.0 - 19.9	0.85	0.48	1.33
20.0 - 49.9	0.88	0.32	1.19
50.0 + up			

SOURCE: Securities and Exchange Commission.

On the one hand, the registration of publicly traded securities along with their sale through well-known underwriters serves an important function. It provides a wealth of trustworthy and easily acquirable information to prospective suppliers of funds. This facilitates the flow of funds to public security markets and makes investors more certain of the expected return for each investment. It also reduces the risk premiums—i.e., lowers capital costs—that larger enterprises must pay in acquiring capital.

However, to the extent that the process does not provide this service at the least possible cost to small and medium-sized firms trying to sell securities, then ventures that otherwise could gain access to public markets (or pay less for transactions in them) will suffer. Jobs and tax revenues will not be generated.

In a recent decision, the SEC itself has acknowledged that these regulations may be unnecessarily burdensome to small firms. It initiated an experimental program that will allow concerns with assets less than $1 million to use a simplified registration process. Under this method they can raise up to $5 million in the public market (*Business Week,* 5/7/79). This will complement the already existing Regulation A, which exempts offerings of less than $1.5 million by companies held by a small number of sophisticated investors from registration requirements.

In the following chapters we will suggest opportunities for state intervention to reduce these transactions and information-providing costs faced by precisely the small, young enterprises that create new jobs and generate new revenues.

Should new or young enterprises surmount the information-and-transaction-cost hurdle, they may still face more serious obstacles. These derive from the particular needs and preferences of institutional investors who have come to dominate the public bond and stock markets. Of the $34.9 billion of net corporate bond purchases in 1977, insurance companies bought $18.3 billion, private corporate pension funds $5.3 billion, and state and local pension funds $4.1 billion (Light and White, 1979). Virtually all of the bonds purchased by the insurance companies are private placements (of which more will be said), thus the public bond markets are dominated by the pension funds.

In the stock market the dominance of institutional investors is even more overwhelming. Since the early 1960s, new purchases of stock each year by these institutional investors have exceeded the net new equity issues of companies. Corporate pension funds have been especially crucial; in the 1970s they have bought more than half of all new equity issues. The growing size of institutional investors, particularly pension funds, reflects a combination of demographic trends, workers' desire for a retirement income beyond Social Security, and the tax advantages of these forms of saving.

The increasing supply of funds to public capital markets through these large, institutionalized financial intermediaries has had a serious impact on the receptiveness of these markets to new and young companies. According to a report by the SBA Task Force on Venture and Equity Capital, "the market value of a firm must be over $100 million to interest pension fund managers" (SBA, 1977).

Based largely on their reading of legal responsibilities imposed by the Employee Retirement Income Security Act of 1974 (ERISA) and other legislation, pension fund managers tend to focus on the larger and more well-known enterprises seeking capital. ERISA, as well as similar state and local laws governing public pensions, was created to end unfair treatment of pension plan members and misuse of pension funds. Many observers believe, however, that these laws have also made pension fund managers excessively risk averse. ERISA forces pension fund managers to comply with a "prudent man" rule of investment and places personal liability on fund managers. In a test case, *Bank of New York vs. Spitzer,* the courts have interpreted this rule to mean that just because the total portfolio of a firm performs well, a trustee is not insulated from personal liability with respect to particular investments (Korchot, 1977).

This emphasis on the risk of individual securities lifted out of the context of the total portfolio, rather than on the contribution of the individual security to the risk of a diversified portfolio, is at odds with principles of efficient investment management. Modern portfolio theory suggests that the total risk of an individual security can be divided into two parts: a part that is correlated with the movement of the market as a whole and a part that is random. The random component can be nearly fully diversified away in a large portfolio, but present regulations of pension fund investments do not admit this possibility. In other words, the courts have failed to recognize the market-perfecting mechanism of risk pooling.

Small and young companies bear the brunt of intensifed pension fund risk aversion since they tend to be the more risky investments. Nonetheless, a well-diversified portfolio would hold shares in these firms and be rewarded with a higher rate of return. If the "prudent man" rule is applied to each investment on its own, however, pension fund managers cannot help but shy away from them. A survey conducted in July 1976 by the International Foundation of Employee Benefit Plans asked whether ERISA affected investment patterns. Of the respondents, 64 percent either agreed somewhat or strongly agreed that "as a result of ERISA our trustees are less willing to invest in anything other than blue chip type investments" (SBA, 1978). Martin Horwitz, chairman and chief executive officer of UV industries, summed up the situation declaring, "The conclusion is inescapable that large amounts of investment money are being managed primarily to avoid liability for the managers. Redlining so-called second-tier [smaller] companies to accomplish this purpose comes down to one result: limiting the flow of investment capital to a small segment of American industry (Horwitz, 1976).

In response to the negative impact ERISA has had on small firms trying to go public, the Department of Labor recently issued an amended regulation under the Act more favorable to such enterprises (DOL, 1979). It allows an investment to be judged with regard to its role in an overall portfolio, not just in terms of its risk standing alone. To what degree this change will aid small business is still uncertain. Independent of ERISA's impact, the concentration of investment decision-making in a relatively small number of institutions supports a conventional wisdom biased against smaller, less glamorous firms (Timbers, 1977). In addition, many public employee pension funds still face significant legal constraints to investing in smaller companies.

Just as concentration on the supply side in public capital markets has produced problems for small and young businesses, so has concentration in the securities industry serving as middleman in the flow of funds. Between 1956 and April 1978 the number of brokerage houses fell from 646 to 505. Since 1973 the market share of the top 25 brokerage houses in terms of commission revenues has climbed from 37.5 percent to 57 percent (West, 1978).

The major force pushing this contraction has been the gradual switch from fixed commission rates to negotiated rates, mandated by the SEC. With fixed commission rates, prices for brokerage services were set by the New York Stock Exchange at a non-competitive level that ensured the existence of many smaller brokers. Since these rates have become deregulated, the larger brokers have effectively taken advantage of the economies of scale in the securities industry and driven out the smaller houses. The watershed came on May 1, 1975 when commissions began to be completely negotiated. Contraction in the industry has tended to be concentrated in those "regional" or "specialty" brokerage houses which have historically been the principal source for underwriting the capital needs of young, small firms.

This bodes ill for these enterprises in two ways. First, these regional and specialty brokers often specialized in selling new securities issues of young, small firms to prospective investors, reducing the *transaction* costs of going to the public market.

Second, regional houses have historically had the best information available on smaller, regional companies since their principals often know regional company management and have been following those companies since their birth. Thus they can reduce *information* costs for prospective investors in these enterprises. Securities and Exchange Commission Chairman Harold Williams foresees the "danger that many regional brokerage firms which have historically served real purposes and helped smaller companies in their areas might disappear in great numbers" (Mullaney, 1978).

This contraction in regional and specialty houses comes at a time when the larger brokers are cutting back on their research. According to David Baker, approximately 500 companies have lost regular analysis and coverage by Wall Street researchers over the past two years. Smaller enterprises get dropped first because the smaller size of their bond and stock issues combined with the biases of institutional investors means the investment houses cannot make as much money facilitating trading in them.

While any one of the obstacles just outlined would be a sufficient barrier to public market financing of small and young enterprises, they typically occur not singly, but together. The following table shows the increasing difficulty of such firms in the public market for equity.

Private Markets

In contrast to public capital markets, private markets are generally more suited and receptive to the financing needs of small and young enterprises. But the benefits these markets afford firms in terms of greater capital availability are accompanied by certain costs. Many of these costs can be interpreted as market imperfections and unjustifiable obstacles to economic development. The major private markets—direct placement of debt with insurance companies, direct placement of equity securities with venture capital companies, and commercial bank loans—

Table 3
Offerings and Money Raised for Companies with New Worth of $5 Million or Less*

Year	Number of Offerings	Total Amount (millions)
1969	548	$1,457.7
1970	209	383.7
1971	224	551.5
1972	418	918.2
1973	69	137.5
1974	8	13.1
1975	4	16.2
1976	not available	145.0
1977	not available	118.0

*Total assets will generally be at least twice a company's net worth.
SOURCE: SBA, 1977; Gumpert, 1979.

represent possible areas of state policy intervention to correct capital market imperfections and stimulate job and revenue creation.

Insurance Company Placements: For those companies that either cannot or do not want to sell bonds in the open public market, there is the alternative of a direct placement of debt—that is, selling a security to no more than twelve or so knowledgeable investors. There are several advantages to this for a small or medium-sized firm. First, direct placements are exempt from the procedures of security registration of the S.E.C. that make the cost of going to the public market prohibitive for smaller issues. Second, since the sale of the security is seldom underwritten by middleman investment houses, much of this cost can be avoided as well. Table 4 illustrates the lower transaction costs attainable through a direct placement.

Instead of SEC registration and investment underwriters being responsible for supplying reliable information to the supplier of funds, direct contact and negotiation takes place between the enterprise trying to obtain funds and the supplier. Because the supplier of capital is acquiring either the entire debt issue the company is trying to sell, or a major portion of it, it has the incentive to do the necessary specialized research and information gathering. Because the terms of security payment are not the standard ones of the public bond market, the supplier of funds can make special requirements of the enterprise to reduce the risk of default. Virtually all of these direct placements of corporate bonds are with life insurance companies. They can tolerate the illiquidity of an investment that cannot be resold (as direct placements cannot under SEC rules), since their cash outflows to policy holders are quite predictable.

Clearly the direct placement corporate bond market is more open than public markets are to small and medium-sized enterprises. The average size of direct placements is one-third the average size of public offerings, and only about 20 percent of directly placed debt issues exceed $4 million—although that 20 percent makes up a disproportionate share of the total dollar volume for direct placements (Brealy and Myers, 1979).

Table 4
A Study of Debt Issues Between 1947 and 1950 Shows
That Issue Costs Are Less for Private Placements
Than for Public Ones

Issue Size ($ million)	Underwriting (Percent)	Other Expenses (Percent)	Total Percent
Private Placements			
0 - 499	1.7%	1.1%	2.8%
500 - 999	1.4	.9	2.3
1000 - 2999	.9	.5	1.4
3000 - 4999	.6	.4	1.0
5000 - 9999	.6	.3	.9
10,000 - 24,999	.3	.3	.6
25,000 - above	.2	.2	.4
Public Issues			
0 - 499	7.3%	2.9%	10.2%
500 - 999	5.5	3.2	8.7
1000 - 2999	3.5	2.1	5.6
3000 - 4999	1.4	1.3	2.7
5000 - 9999	.9	1.0	1.9
10,000 - 24,999	1.0	.7	1.7
25,000 - above	.7	.4	1.1

SOURCE: Brealy and Myers (1979).

The direct placement imposes its own special burdens, however. Although good data are not available to determine exactly the interest premium that must be paid to a supplier of funds in the direct placement market, most observers estimate it to be at least .5 percent. Moreover, besides being able to demand this interest premium, the insurance companies—ten companies account for 55 percent to 65 percent of all direct placements annually—can impose numerous requirements that limit the freedom and flexibility of the borrowing firm while the debt is still outstanding. Although this protects the insurance company, it may make it more difficult for the small or young firm to do business.

Finally, and most important from a public policy standpoint, although direct placements definitely serve a smaller size enterprise than the public bond market, the firms served are generally still fairly large companies. Many of the larger insurance companies, especially the top ten, who do two-thirds of all private placements, will not give funds to an enterprise with less than $200 million in sales, at least ten years of favorable operating experience, and a debt/equity ratio of no more than 0.6 (White and Light, 1979; Moore, 1979). In 1977, for example, John Hancock made one loan to one firm below $100 in sales. That firm controlled 70 percent of its world market in a "safe industry," paper information storage. The lender nevertheless felt constrained to impose a very heavy penalty clause for prepayment to cover its high information and transaction costs. This kind of investment activity excludes virtually 100 percent of those young, small firms that economic development policy should be designed to encourage.

Venture Capital: Corresponding to the direct placement market for debt dominated by insurance companies is a direct placement market for equity securities known as the venture capital market. This market is of fairly recent origin, and those supplying capital in it range from private venture capital investment firms, venture capital divisions of large corporations, closed-end investment companies, family (including the Rockefellers and Whitneys) investment companies, and such federally licensed institutions as Small Business Investment Companies (SBICs) and so-called Minority Enterprise SBICs (MESBICs). Taken together, there are between 500 and 600 separate institutions involved in direct placement or equity financing.

Just as insurance companies assume responsibility for research and information gathering on prospective sellers of directly placed debt securities, venture capital firms screen proposals from enterprises in which they may purchase a sizable equity share. These are typically small and young firms unable to seek funds in the public equity market for the reasons outlined above.

Venture capital firms provide initial equity capital and second and third round financing with the expectation that the firm will grow, making the venture capitalist's share in the firm increasingly valuable. Here, however, a problem arises that has stifled the development of the direct placement equity market in contrast to the direct placement debt market. To cash in on its capital gain, a venture capital firm has to be able to sell its share of the enterprise to someone, usually after three to seven years. This is not a problem with directly placed debt, since the borrower pays off a fixed sum in interest and principal over time. The easiest way for a venture capital firm to cash in on its investments would be for the company it holds to start selling equity securities in the public market. Then the venture capital firm can be paid off in stock that can be resold in the open market to other investors.

Unfortunately, venture capital firms have been caught in the paradox that one of the major reasons they exist—the difficulty of small and young firms going public—is one of the main reasons they have trouble making money from the directly placed equity they buy. Consequently, the direct placement equity market is not serving as an adequate source of funds for small and young corporations. Its total assets have been estimated at only $1.7 billion; annual investment is only slightly over $100 *million* (out of an entire capital market that has $380 *billion* for new investment annually).

Because of this double bind, the suppliers of venture capital are putting more and more of their funds into older companies having a better chance of succeeding in the public issues market. In 1975, only 5 percent of the venture capital industry's new investments went to start-ups of new enterprises and only 2 percent to first round financings (SBA, 1977). According to the SBA Task Force on Venture and Equity Capital, "This steady shift towards a more conservative investment policy comes from perceived difficulty in recycling investment funds as restrictions on the access of small and growing business to the public securities market has become more costly and difficult."

Commercial Bank Debt: Faced with impediments to seeking debt financing in the public bond and direct placement markets, together with barriers to acquiring equity financing in stock and venture capital markets, small and young enterprises frequently turn to commercial banks. Obtaining a loan from a commercial bank in essence amounts to a direct placement of debt.

Banks are well suited to serving a population of smaller and more diverse borrowers, to which growing businesses belong. The importance of commercial bank loans to smaller firms can be seen in the following table.

A firm in the $5 million to $10 million asset range is about four times as likely as one in the $250 million to $1,000 million range to obtain a dollar of debt capital from a bank as opposed to some other source. Since dependence on bank loans stems from a "captive relationship" between banks and small enterprises, this form of financing carries with it certain burdens.

Generally, small and young corporations find themselves restricted

Table 5
Ratio of Bank Loans to Other Long-Term Debt
for Manufacturing Firms *(second quarter 1977)*

Asset Size of Enterprise (millions of dollars)

5 - 10	.978
10 - 25	1.100
25 - 50	.734
50 - 100	.569
100 - 250	.358
250 - 1000	.254
over 1000	.112
all	.253

SOURCE: Federal Trade Commission.

to local banking markets. For example, firms with total assets of $1 million or less receive about 90 percent of their loans from banks in the same SMSA (Griggs and Petty, 1972). A major reason for this is that the value of a loan will not merit the requisite on-site inspection and negotiation on the part of more distant regional banks, nor does it merit general, widespread publication of information about the business as in public markets. For local banks, however, the information and transaction costs are significantly lower.

Unfortunately, local banking markets tend to be characterized by a high degree of concentration (Tally, 1977). In some states, such as Georgia, Arkansas, Montana and Kentucky, approximately one-half of all counties have only one or two banks (Daniels and Kieschnick, 1978). In contrast, scores of large banks operating on an international, national or regional scale compete quite aggressively among themselves, but only for those much larger firms that have both lower information and transaction costs and much lower perceived risks.

Often this market concentration is thought to lead to higher interest rates. While this is true, most research has found that the increase in interest rates is small (Heggestad, 1979). Far more important is the effect on the availability of capital. Banks in concentrated markets trade off monopoly profits at a normal risk level, for normal profits at a below-normal risk level. As the famous British economist Hicks observed, "The best of all monopoly profits is the quiet life." The result is that funds are allocated to borrowing firms not on the basis of the interest rate they are willing and able to pay, but on the basis of loan size and risk. In essence, below a certain size or above a certain risk level, no increase in the interest rate paid would cause the bank to supply a loan. Clearly this credit rationing limits the amount of business loans made in the local market and increases the proportion of low-risk assets like Treasury bills in bank portfolios. This works to the detriment of independent, young businesses.

The fact that market concentration affects the risk-taking behavior of banks has been confirmed in a number of studies. Gardner, in a study of St. Louis (1973), and Heggestad, in a comparative analysis of several metropolitan areas (1977), have both found credit rationing to take place in a way which lowers the risk to the bank, rather than raising the return. These studies in urban areas are supported by similar studies in isolated rural banking markets by Fraser and Rose (1971), Chandross (1971) and McCall and Peterson (1977). They all found that the entry of a new bank into a county with few banks resulted in dramatic changes in the existing banks' portfolios. Funds were shifted from low risk securities such as public bonds, to riskier assets such as commercial loans. McCall and Peterson also found that the banks that were there in the first place were not financially hurt by the entry of the new one—indicating that the riskier loans were still viable ones.

Independent of problems associated with banking market concentration, small businesses would expect to have trouble raising money from commercial banks. Because of market imperfections already described, these firms often have too large a proportion of their assets financed by previous debt and too little by the owners' contribution of capital, equity. Banks view this high debt/equity ratio negatively for two reasons. First, it increases the likelihood of financial distress—the business may have difficulty meeting debt service payments, or actually default on the payments. This reflects the fact that a high debt/equity ratio means a large, fixed portion of the firm's current income is already obligated to paying off past creditors. Thus it is more probable that the firm could have insufficient income left over to make payments on new loans. Secondly, the equity base is important in terms of collateral requirements. A bank typically asks for a borrower to pledge some collateral that can be claimed in the case of default. Usually this collateral is some of the fixed assets owned by the firm, that is, equity. Finally, even if the bank does not anticipate having to liquidate that collateral, it protects the bank's position. If the borrower's assets are already tied up as collateral to the bank, they will not be able to be used to obtain additional debt from some other lender.

Moreover, whether a borrower can provide collateral provides an easy measure of legitimacy of the credit applicant.

It seems reasonable to say that excessive dependence of small firms on commercial banks is no better for the banks than it is for the firms. But as Table 6 shows, that is precisely the state to which capital market imperfections have brought us.

Table 6
Sources of Funds for Manufacturing Corporations by Size: 1950-1971 and 1972-1976 Averages
(size in $ millions, Figures in percent)

Size	All	1	1-5	5-10	10-25	25-50	50-100	100-250	250-1000	over 1000
Retained Earnings										
58-71	34.05	29.75	30.23	30.24	19.19	19.22	19.23	32.50	34.18	35.83
72-76	45.50	48.87	32.55	34.22	38.47	44.50	47.29	42.50	40.42	49.18
Capital Stock										
58-71	12.19	5.13	2.53	7.40	6.70	11.30	8.17	9.84	9.86	14.09
72-76	8.47	-5.78	7.56	5.25	6.39	4.20	-3.07	8.04	11.00	9.53
Other S.T. Liabilities										
58-71	12.95	13.49	11.39	9.75	7.93	12.16	11.25	9.76	13.31	1.350
72-76	16.22	19.63	16.70	18.13	17.44	15.26	17.41	24.17	17.58	14.89
Trade Debt										
58-71	8.34	16.56	20.90	18.38	18.29	13.58	11.00	9.50	7.57	6.84
72-76	8.29	11.23	18.11	16.25	13.66	12.94	12.39	8.89	8.38	5.96
Short-Term Bank Loans										
58-71	5.28	7.33	8.21	10.50	11.66	9.86	9.28	8.25	6.63	3.93
72-76	2.87	1.59	7.86	7.75	4.33	-1.30	.71	-7.79	-8.57	-3.85
Long Term Bank Loans										
58-71	4.80	11.03	8.75	8.78	12.59	10.60	10.65	8.64	6.26	3.01
72-76	3.93	22.27	9.21	8.12	11.25	13.17	12.76	5.45	6.67	.62
Other Long Term Liabilities										
58-71	22.39	16.75	18.00	14.94	23.64	23.28	30.40	21.51	22.18	22.79
72-76	20.46	8.01	10.29	8.46	11.23	12.52	18.73	24.52	23.67	

SOURCE: Daniels and Kieschnick (1978).

Assessing the Overall Impact on Small Enterprise

On the whole, small firms have higher debt/equity ratios, reflecting their difficulty in raising equity capital, through either the public market or venture capitalists. Their debt financing differs as well, being shorter in term (note the high composition of trade debt and short-term loans) and when long term, more often from banks as opposed to the private placement sources. Small firms' lack of access to equity capital and long-term debt must be juxtaposed with data from a preliminary study (Kieschnick and Daniels, 1978) showing that as a group these businesses offered a competitive return adjusted for risk. Attractive but capital-starved small firms frequently must merge with larger corporations as a way out of their dilemma. For example, during 1976 acquisition of firms under $1 million in assets accounted for 76.1 percent of all acquisitions. And the $1 million to $9.9 million asset size class accounted for 11.5 percent of all acquisitions (FTC, 1976).

In summary, although states devote almost 100 percent of their development finance efforts to encourage and promote the setting up of new plants, subsidiaries and headquarters offices by known, large firms, these firms account for only about one-half of new job creation and do *not* face capital market problems. It is those young, small, growing firms that account for the other 50 percent of new jobs. These firms are rarely counted, and are usually ignored by state development finance efforts. Yet they are the very ones that must contend with capital market imperfections.

HOUSING FINANCE The growth of markets and labor supply are critical to state and local economies. Both of these development determinants are, as we have noted, rooted in a common source—the location—and migration—of population. The movement of households, particularly within metropolitan areas, in part depends on the cost and availability of housing. Since a large portion of the funds used to construct or purchase housing are borrowed, the efficiency and equity of capital markets in financing housing will influence all other dimensions of an area's economic development.

Residential housing in the United States is financed primarily through mortgages. Residential mortgages represent debt instruments backed by the collateral of real estate. Obtaining debt financing for housing entails many of the problems associated with obtaining debt financing for small business. As financial securities go, residential mortgages are quite small. Moreover, the kinds of real estate being financed are diverse and the terms required for a loan (by both borrower and lender) are not standard. This means that households must rely on local sources of credit for mortgages. Local financial intermediaries represent the only ones in a position to originate and service the mortgage: transaction and information costs for more distant regional or national sources would be substantially higher.

These attributes of housing finance would suggest that the cost and availability of capital for this good would vary substantially by region and that households in concentrated financial market areas would suffer from the same credit rationing and high interest rates affecting small business. In fact, housing finance *has* suffered from localism in funds and credit rationing (usually in the form of requirements for larger downpayments by more risky household borrowers) (Grebler, 1977).

However, innovation in capital markets through private and public institutions such as GNMA and FNMA has reduced these imperfections. The chief result has been the development of a secondary market for residential mortgages that allows housing to be financed in the national capital markets at the same time as local credit sources originate and service these debt instruments. Mortgage companies came on the scene to specialize in originating mortgages for resale to other, more distant investors. The specialization of mortgage companies permitted them to develop a reputation among secondary buyers as a trustworthy evaluator of credit applications and certifier of quality. More recently (in the 1960s), private mortgage insurers began to be licensed, further reducing default risk to those who purchased mortgages in the secondary market.

Thrift institutions (savings and loan associations and mutual savings banks) and commercial banks are the largest originators and holders of residential mortgages in the country, accounting for 77.6 percent of originations and 78.2 percent of holdings. The bulk of both originations and holdings come from thrift institutions.

While the specialization of thrift institutions in housing finance has made the mortgage market more efficient in many ways, it has also given rise to a major problem in the supply of mortgage funds. As one would expect, the portfolios of thrift institutions are dominated by mortgages. This makes it difficult for thrift institutions to compete for the deposits of households, their basic source of funds, during periods when interest rates are rising. Since mortgages have fixed yields and take a number of years to pay off, the return that thrifts earn on their portfolios is quite insensitive to increases in the market interest rate in the short term. To compete effectively with other potential investments for household funds, they would have to raise the interest rates they pay depositors. Unable to do this as a result of their dependence on mortgage assets, the thrifts lose some deposits to competitors like Treasury bills and other open market securities whose return rises with market interest rates. This process of loss of funds in thrifts is known as *disintermediation,* and can severely curtail the amount of capital available to finance residential mortgages.

Recently, two private market innovations have emerged that have begun to correct these housing capital market imperfections. One of these innovations affects the uses of funds for thrift institutions, the other affects the sources of funds. The variable rate mortgage, now being widely tested in California, permits the yield on thrift institutions' outstanding mortgages to rise with market interest rates. Thrifts can use these increased yields to pay interest on the negotiable certificates of deposit (CDs) they increasingly issue to compete for funds with commercial bank CDs, commercial paper and U.S. Treasury bills.

The emergence of these private and Federal innovations over recent years suggests that single-family house mortgage markets are working reasonably efficiently. The major exception may be the lower-income home owner in lower-income neighborhoods of central cities. Although the practice of "redlining," in which banks are alleged to have disqualified whole neighborhoods of central cities from receiving home mortgages, has been widely debated, there has been very little reliable research analyzing the extent of this practice. In one recent study of thousands of mortgages in New York state, researchers found a few instances of the redlining of whole communities, and widespread evidence of systematic discrimination by race irrespective of location (Shafer, 1978).

State banking commissioners could be of great assistance in data collection and analysis to further our understanding of this issue. In the meantime, it appears that there is at least a market failure generated by racial discrimination in which banks presume that race stands for creditworthiness—or not—irrespective of whether a more careful investment in information about a specific borrower would support that pre-judgment. It may also be true that the kind of pre-judgment extends to certain kinds of dwellings or certain kinds of neighborhoods without a more careful investment in information to determine the underlying soundness of the home owner or housing stock.

PUBLIC INFRASTRUCTURE FINANCE

Private economic activity requires public infrastructure. Both underdeveloped, lagging areas and developed but distressed areas often suffer from an inadequate infrastructure. In the former case this means starting from scratch, as the Economic Development Administration has done with its program of road building and general construction in areas like Appalachia. In the latter case this means modernization of often obsolete metropolitan highways and transit, airports, public utilities and land, as has been attempted with HUD's urban redevelopment programs. A miniscule portion of this local infrastructure, however, is financed by federal government grant-in-aid programs such as EDA or HUD (Haar and Lewis, 1971).

Just as a private corporation must finance its investment projects, so must state and local governments pay for their capital expenditures. While a significant portion of public infrastructure projects may be paid out for current tax revenues, between 1958 and 1973 approximately 40 percent of all state and local capital outlays were financed by long-term debt (Light and White, 1979). The use of debt to pay for public infrastructure allows the different generations of users who benefit from the projects over their lifetimes to shoulder the cost—as opposed to it falling entirely on current taxpayers.

Virtually all long-term debt financing for state and local government is acquired in the tax-exempt bond market. The unique characteristic of this market is that the interest paid to purchasers of these bonds cannot be taxed by the Federal government, and often not by the state or local governments either.

Problems in this tax-exempt bond market may eventually result in reduced capital spending or increased taxes and user charges. These problems arise both from capital market imperfections and from the special nature of the demand for state and local bonds arising from their tax exemption.

While the tax exempt bond market is essentially a public capital market, it has many features ill-suited to the indirect relationship between security issuers and buyers that typifies such a market. First, far from being standard and homogeneous, the tax-exempt bond issues tend to be very complicated and diverse. A single bond issue may have as many as 30 different maturities within it and 12 different coupon rates, or some combination of these terms. Second, detailed and reliable information is not provided buyers in any way comparable to the practices of public corporate bond and equity markets. Tax-exempt bonds are also exempt from the security registration provisions of the Securities Act of 1933. The information provided by tax-exempt bond issuers normally relates more to the legality of their procedures in approving the issue than to the financial condition of the state or locality.

In the absence of good credit information being supplied by the governmental units who want to sell bonds, credit rating agencies have sprung up—namely, Moody's and Standard and Poor's. Yet the value of this rating has been limited because the basis on which bonds are rated is not generally known by investors, and because smaller issues of bonds are sometimes simply not rated (Forbes and Petersen, 1976).

These market imperfections tend to be compounded by the relatively small size of tax-exempt bond issues. On average they are only one-fourth the size of new corporate offerings (Petersen, 1974).

This limitation has two direct effects. First, since many transaction costs, such as bond counsel and basic underwriting fees, are fixed, the cost of raising state and local debt is higher than if the issues were packaged in larger amounts. Second, for institutional investors, the larger the number of different securities owned, the greater the cost of portfolio management. An entire issue of state or local bonds may not be large enough to fit into one of these portfolios.

Offsetting these obstacles for tax-exempt bond issues is the major advantage of their tax exemption, which permits state and local borrowers to sell bonds at a lower rate of interest—65 percent to 75 percent of the rate for long-term corporate bonds.

Yet this very tax exemption has imposed its own burdens. At these lower yields, the bonds are only attractive to investors who are taxed at a comparatively high rate—commercial banks, high income households, and casualty insurance companies.

Obviously, these tax-exempt bonds are of no interest to large and growing tax-exempt institutions such as corporate pension funds, local and state employee pension funds, union pension funds, churches, university endowments or private foundations. These large institutional investors have no taxable income against which to take the municipal tax credit.

As of 1977, commercial banks held $118 billion in tax-exempt bonds, households held $77 billion, and casualty insurance companies held $47 billion (Light and White, 1979). But as commercial banks have developed other tax shelters, such as leasing activities and foreign tax credits, their interest in state and local debt has waned; while purchasing 68 percent of new issues in the 1960s, they accounted for only 30 percent during 1972-76.

This has been compensated for to some limited extent by households pushed into higher tax brackets by recent rapid inflation. Yet there are problems in the continued reliance on households as a source of tax-exempt bond demand. High minimum purchase requirements (the standard is $5000) often make it difficult for household investors to buy tax-exempts and still maintain a diversified portfolio. The absence of sound public information about these securities often makes it difficult for households to evaluate potential state and local bond investments. And the absence of an active secondary market for some tax-exempt bonds make them a comparatively illiquid security.

These problems may in part have been remedied by legislation passed in 1976 that allowed the sale of mutual funds that invest in tax-exempt bonds.

Each of the three areas in which there is a legitimate reason for state intervention in capital markets—support for the creation and expansion of new or young growing, profitable small firms; housing finance; and infrastructure development—is an area in which significant innovation has occurred at the state level. Whether or not it exists in other critical areas of governmental activity, in the field of economic development finance Federalism lives!

Chapter 4 outlines a means of evaluating state intervention in capital markets in light of the needs outlined in this chapter. Chapters 5, 6 and 7 will describe and critique the innovations themselves.

4
GOALS AND TOOLS: FORMS OF STATE INTERVENTION IN CAPITAL MARKETS

While knowledge of goods market and capital market forces that give rise to state economic development problems is a necessary condition for formulating effective policy, it is by no means sufficient. The other major, and still missing piece of information—possible methods for doing something about these problems—will be explored in the remainder of our study. Our analysis so far has pointed to two fundamental approaches to intervention in the development process through capital market policies.

First, the availability of capital is a pre-condition for any economic enterprise. In some cases economic activity that could occur does not because of capital market imperfections. This presents each state government with a valuable opportunity. If it can correct or counteract the problems that produce underfinancing of viable small businesses, housing and public infrastructure enterprises, then additional employment and growth will occur in the state.

Second, the cost of capital enters into the overall costs of production for an enterprise. *In theory,* the cost of capital could be depressed to balance out other production costs or market disadvantages in a state or substate area. Thus even though the cost of capital normally does not represent an important determinant of where job-creating investment takes place, it might be manipulated to influence industrial location. Both practical and political considerations will severely limit the usefulness of this approach in American states.

In this chapter we lay out a framework for thinking about these two approaches. This framework is then applied in Chapter 5 through 8. At this point we want to make sure that state policymakers understand what questions should be asked about intervention in capital markets before delving more deeply into working models of business, housing and public infrastructure financing.

ASKING THE RIGHT QUESTIONS Effective state economic development policy causes jobs and income to be created when they would not otherwise be. Any policy that proposes to accomplish this feat should be subjected to several questions. First, since the policy intends to add employment that otherwise would not exist in the state, where do the jobs come from? Second, what does this policy cost? Has the full range of costs to be avoided properly been accounted for? Third, what are the appropriate tools the state could use to trigger these jobs? The other critical questions—how well has the policy performed in other places and, how might it be improved upon?—will be introduced here and developed in chapters 5 through 8.

Where Do the Jobs Come From?

Consider first a policy which makes capital available to an enterprise offering a competitive risk-adjusted return but previously denied funds due to capital market imperfections. In the most immediate sense, the jobs are produced by the newly funded enterprise through new employment resulting from the firm's birth or expansion. But the capital supplied to the firm had to come from somewhere. It may have been shifted away from another enterprise, in which case at least some of the new jobs merely represent employment *displaced* from somewhere else.

If the capital comes at the expense of another enterprise within the state, there will be a new employment or total income gain *only* if the firms to which the funds get shifted can use them more productively. Based on what we know of the often superior, but unacknowledged return on small enterprise, this gain will frequently occur if the newly financed enterprise is a young, small firm rather than a larger, more mature firm.

From a state's perspective, it would obviously be more attractive for the financing to come, perhaps in some indirect fashion, at the expense of a firm in another state or outside the country entirely. Then all the jobs generated by the newly financed enterprise will represent a net addition to the state's economy.

Finally, if the capital that the state channels to viable but capital-poor enterprises comes from income that would have gone to consumption—as in the case of consumption-tax financed state direct loan programs—no investment anywhere will be directly displaced, although there may be some indirect reduction if households' savings are reduced in response to lower after-tax income.

Not all the jobs created by firms financed through a state capital-market perfecting development policy will be truly new jobs for the nation as a whole, nor even new jobs for that state. Some employment will be displaced in the process. *But* it is not necessary that jobs just be shifted around. Employment gains for every state (and thus for the nation as a whole) can be achieved without diverting investment from other states. Displacement between states can be avoided simply by shifting funds within a state from less productive enterprises to more productive, but underfunded, young small firms.

In contrast, consider a policy which makes capital available to certain firms, not suffering from capital unavailability, at below market rates in order to make their location or expansion in certain areas more attractive. This approach can *only* produce jobs at the expense of another state, or in the best and unlikely case, at the expense of some economic activity outside the country. Such a policy will both provoke retaliation as well as cost state governments much more than they can afford to pay.

What Does the Policy Cost?

Too often, state policy makers have rushed in with ill-considered interventions which create more public burden than benefit. Some proposed solutions to economic development problems via the capital market simply will not work at all, while others achieve their goals only at an exorbitant public cost. A state government should consider three kinds of costs when evaluating any plan.

Most obviously, intervention may require spending increasingly scarce tax dollars; these public funds have alternative uses. A dollar misspent on loan subsidies means one less dollar available for public clinics or aid to secondary education.

In addition to these opportunity costs, raising the necessary tax dollars means transferring income from taxpayers to someone else. This may have undesirable effects on the distribution of income, especially if the recipient of the transfer turns out to be a large creditworthy corporation that needs neither credit nor subsidy, and would have made the same investment decision without the gift of taxpayers' money.

Finally, at a less obvious level, new economic inefficiencies may well be a side effect of attempts to remedy existing development problems. It is very important to understand that too often in the past government interventions in capital markets, while correcting some flaws, have made others worse.

What Are the Appropriate Tools the State Could Use to Trigger These Jobs?

To this question we will devote most of the remainder of Chapter 4. The key dimension of any capital market intervention will be whether it makes capital available in a market-perfecting way or merely manipulates the cost of capital in attempt to displace firms from one place to another. Yet beyond this central issue lie important details of intervention. For example, does the policy rely on regulation of private financial institutions in the state, either administratively or through the use of more explicit economic incentives? Or does it employ some kind of direct financial intermediation by the state?

FROM QUESTIONS TO ANSWERS

Whether making capital available to underfinanced firms or reducing its costs to others, a state is faced with altering the normal operations of capital markets. In doing so it has three alternatives. It can influence the allocation and pricing of capital by existing private financial intermediaries through its power to regulate these institutions. It can influence the allocation and pricing behavior of private financial institutions through offering certain economic incentives. Or it can establish state financial intermediaries designed to make the desired financings directly.

In practice, many states have chosen to use a combination of these three instruments. This reflects the fact that each is best suited for particular situations. We will first describe the potential and pitfalls of each of these tools in general terms in this chapter. This description will set the stage for describing and evaluating actual instruments and institutions to carry out specific state economic development tasks in succeeding chapters.

ADMINISTRATIVE REGULATION OF STATE FINANCIAL INTERMEDIARIES

Perhaps the most obvious tool for making private capital markets perform according to public policy is administrative regulation. After all, a large proportion of the financial intermediaries in any state will be chartered by the state government. To obtain and maintain their charters, they must conform to certain rules governing their sources and uses of funds and the means by which they compete with other banks. In theory, this chartering and rule setting authority gives state government a direct means of leverage over which enterprises get capital from these institutions and what price different users pay for financing.

In reality, however, the state's influence is limited by the fact that neither all capital markets, nor all financial intermediaries in certain sectors of capital markets, are subject to its regulation. In some major sectors, such as public capital markets, the state plays virtually no role. In fact, public stock and bond capital markets have the extensive fluidity which defines their character precisely because they are regulated not by the fifty states, but federally. In other important sectors, such as commercial banking or thrift institutions, state chartering and regulation play a major regulatory function. Still, the state shares this responsibility with the federal government, which almost wholly regulates federally chartered banks and even regulates some aspects of many state chartered institutions.

Obviously, the state has no power over financial institutions which it does not charter or which are beyond its borders. Whatever restrictions an individual state imposes on the intermediaries over which it has authority, it must always keep in mind that the assets of those institutions at any time might flow away to other federal or state chartered institutions over which it has no control. There is in fact a good deal of jumping about from one banking regulator to another in order to take advantage of less stringent or less costly regulation. This is a price of our "dual banking system," as it is called, and it works both ways. When big Chase National merged with the much smaller Manhattan Company, the new bank kept the charter of the latter because it was far less constraining. Recently, 10 percent of the bank assets of the Boston Federal Reserve shifted to state chartering in order to avoid the high costs of "Fed" membership. But when an aggressive California banking commissioner began to press for stronger regulations influencing to whom banks could lend, many California banks threatened to shift to Federal charters.

To see more precisely the opportunities *and* limitations of administrative regulation, we must look at which intermediaries the state charters, how it regulates them, and how these regulations can be used to alter capital market conditions.

The largest category of financial institutions regulated by the state are commercial banks. Of the 14,707 commercial banks in the country, 10,053 are state chartered, with the remainder federally chartered. State chartered banks tend to be much smaller than nationally chartered ones; even though they are more numerous, they account for only 45 percent of all bank assets. Virtually all state chartered banks are insured by the Federal Deposit Insurance Corporation and are thus subject to F.D.I.C. regulation as well. Over eleven hundred state banks belong to the Federal Reserve System and must conform with federal policies. The state banks belonging to the federal system tend to be the larger and more important state banks.

Like commercial banks, the majority of thrift institutions (designed to employ funds primarily in financing home mortgages and household credit) are regulated by state governments. Of 5,102 savings and loan associations, 3,042 operate under state charter. But the assets held by the state chartered savings and loans are not proportionate to their number; more than half of all savings and loan assets are in federally chartered institutions. All of the 480 mutual savings banks, primarily in New England and the mid-Atlantic, are state chartered. Of the 22,448 credit unions, 9,696 have state charters. Again, the largest of these tend to be federally chartered.

Both the 3,000 casualty insurance companies and the 1,833 life insurance companies are licensed and regulated by states. State governments also regulate the over 2,000 state and local public employee pension funds. Contrary to banks and thrifts, neither insurance companies nor public pension funds are federally regulated, making them a particularly important target for creative state intervention. Still, there are limits. Overly aggressive taxation and regulation of insurance companies by any one state could lead to a shift of assets, employment and activities to other states.

While each of these financial intermediaries has its own special chartering and regulations, they share a common regulatory framework. Typically, three dimensions of their activities are controlled: liabilities, or sources of funds; assets, or uses of funds; and market structure, or entry and exit into the market. Because a serious discussion of each kind of financial intermediary is not feasible, we will focus our attention on the overwhelmingly important group—commercial banks.

Commercial banks, as we have seen, are the most accessible of all financial institutions to small firms, who bear the greatest burden of capital market imperfection. Where particularly instructive, we will cite other examples involving financial intermediaries.

What kind of regulation is commercial banking subject to and how can these regulations be exploited to correct market failures?

Commercial bank liability regulations specify the terms on which banks can accept deposits—for example, maximum interest rates and withdrawal periods. Asset regulations circumscribe loans and investments—requiring a certain proportion of a bank's assets to be held in non-interest bearing reserve accounts as security, and restricting the types of loans that can be made, the maximum amounts, and the interest rates. Market structure regulations establish the process for authorization of charters for new banks, and for approval of branch locations. National banks are subject to these same branching regulations as well as state banks.

On the face of it, asset regulation would seem to be far more important than liability regulation, since asset regulation directly affects who and what kinds of enterprises can use the assets. But as we shall see in more detail in Chapter 5, liability regulation significantly affects the uses of assets. Or, to put the matter another way, the character and term of the uses of funds are strongly constrained by the character and term of the sources of funds.

As we saw in Chapter 3, commercial banks cannot lend long-term expansion capital to business enterprises with short-term deposits. And venture capital companies which try to invest equity with debt they have borrowed do so at great peril either to themselves or those in whom they invest. Sooner or later something will have to give; when unforseen circumstances arise, either the venture capitalist will be unable to repay its borrowed debt, or will have to make a fatal claim on the firm in which it has invested. Sources of funds must match uses of funds as to both length of term and level of risk if the private financial intermediary is both soundly invested and financially sound.

To date, state regulatory policy concerning liability management has been almost totally inconsiderate of state economic development. In focusing so totally on the safety of deposits and liabilities, banking, thrift and insurance commissioners have encouraged risk aversion in the uses of funds. In fixing ceilings on the prices certain kinds of banks or savings and loans can pay for deposits, regulators have discouraged competition for funds in good times, and encouraged funds to flow out of regulated markets (like housing finance by thrifts) to unregulated markets in bad times (what we call disintermediation). Lack of competition at any time leads, as we have seen, to market control, credit allocation and risk aversion. Disintermediation cuts off funds for lending completely.

What is called for is creative liability regulation which removes barriers to competition on the liability side in order to stimulate more aggressive risk taking on the asset side. As we shall see in the next chapter, this can be done without violating prudence and reducing responsibility.

The most direct regulatory vehicle for influencing the availability or cost of capital, obviously, are rules governing asset holdings. For example, the requirement for holding a certain percentage of assets in reserve may be used either as a carrot or a stick. The "reserve requirement" is the percentage of the demand, savings and time deposits that cannot be invested in earning assets but must be held in the form of reserves. Typically, this is about 3 percent on savings deposits, 3-6 percent on time deposits, and 10-12 percent on demand deposits. A state could place a 100 percent reserve requirement on some fraction of the bank's assets, to be relaxed by the amount loaned to the favored category of investment—such as small firms, or minority owned firms or firms located in depressed areas. Thus, the intermediary would either make an interest paying loan in the desired category or place an equal amount in non-interest bearing reserves (Thurow, 1976). This is the "stick" alternative. Using the "carrot" alternative, the bank could be allowed to offset some of its existing reserve requirements with loans to those same favored asset categories.

The carrot approach, although superficially attractive, is limited by the fact that reserve requirements exist for a good reason—to ensure proper liquidity in commercial banking operations. Moreover, any official offer to reduce reserve requirements may not be very effective, as many bankers would hold at least the equivalent of the required reserves—even in the absence of regulation—out of a sense of what is prudent management.

Problems with the stick approach are even more serious. If required loans or investments are either riskier or less profitable than assets in the current portfolio of commercial banks, then the regulation may have the effect of a tax. It will force those who invest in the regulated financial intermediaries to bear either higher risk or lower return than would otherwise be the case. The financial community, especially those institutions subject to the special regulation, would undoubtedly respond with political pressure to have the costly regulation removed, or to be compensated in some other way. This pressure would be reinforced by the threat that capital will flow away from state commercial banks to federally chartered institutions in the state, or from the state as a whole to places not subject to that form of asset regulation.

The threat is, as we have seen, a credible one. While the power of a state government ends at its borders, the flow of capital does not observe these same boundaries. On the contrary, capital is quite mobile. Many financial institutions participate in buying and selling securities all over the country. This is true of most insurance companies and large banks. Other institutions, which have a strictly local area of operations, nonetheless participate in secondary markets for securities of ve ures from a completely different state or region. Individual investors or depositors can shift their assets to unregulated institutions or markets.

An example of this capital export response can be seen in the effects of Arkansas' usury law. This interest rate ceiling of 10 percent has during high market interest rate periods led Arkansas banks to lending funds they have on deposit with the Federal Reserve to banks in other states, purchasing certificates of deposit in out-of-state banks, and participating in loans made by out-of-state banks. If banks do not export capital through these channels, it becomes more likely that individual depositors will choose to do so on their own. They withdraw their money and buy CDs in out-of-state banks or purchase nationally marketed securities. A survey of Arkansas banks during 1974, when open-market securities paid 12 percent, revealed that nearly $300 million had fled the state. This amount was equal to more than 10 percent of the total loans held by Arkansas banks at that time. The outflow was composed of $145 million in net sales of federal funds, $32 million in bank purchases of certificates of deposit out of state, $61 million in loan participations with out of state banks, $53 million in large time-deposits withdrawn and deposited out of state, and $42 million in small time-deposits withdrawn for purchase of securities (Lynch and Hardin, 1974). Any state government that attempts to direct private investment into higher risk or lower return assets by regulation can count on fostering the export of capital from its state. Not surprisingly, the use of regulatory authority to mandate certain types of lending and investment has been rare.

Regulation does not mean merely *mandating* behavior, however. It can also mean *facilitating* new kinds of lending behavior that will contribute to more efficient capital markets (but that cannot happen without the state's explicit stamp of approval). Here the state's authority to charter new types of intermediaries comes into play. For instance, Business Development Corporations (sometimes also called Development Credit Corporations) now operate in a majority of states. BDCs (or DCCs) were first designed in Maine in 1949 in order to provide a more effective method for channeling capital from existing private financial intermediaries into small business loans. State chartered banks, insurance companies and thrift institutions are empowered to invest in and lend to them. In doing so, many of their usual asset regulations are waived.

This approach has been further refined in the $100 million Massachusetts Capital Resources Corporation (owned collectively by all of the state's $30 billion life insurance companies and empowered to lend to rapidly growing firms both too small and too risky for any single insurance company), the proposed Massachusetts Lending Corporation (to be owned by the state thrift industry), and the recently enacted California Business and Industrial Development Corporations (BIDCOs). Each of these new institutions is designed, in its distinctive way, to reduce information and transaction costs, and to spread and pool risks for young, small, growing firms—thus facilitating investments or loans by participating state chartered financial intermediaries that would not otherwise be possible.

Using regulatory authority to influence capital markets does not necessarily mean creating a new institution, or writing a new rule. It can amount to reviewing and modifying existing regulations that unnecessarily inhibit financing of good enterprises. One possible area for this de-regulation is branching restrictions. In many states, regulations that limit banks to one location (unit banking) or to multiple locations within the home county (restricted branching) contribute substantially to market concentration and a consequent reduction in small business lending.

INFLUENCING FINANCIAL INTERMEDIARIES THROUGH ECONOMIC INCENTIVES

A command-and-control approach to regulating financial intermediaries seems straightforward and easy—until we look more closely at what can happen when a state government administratively orders around institutions and investors owning or controlling large pools of capital. Too often, the regulation can act as a tax on the institution, or offer no real incentive to change investment behavior, or encourage the flight of assets out of state. Where regulations hold more promise, the key factor is usually that they facilitate opportunities for regulated institutions to pursue greater profits.

Obviously, state policy makers need a strategy that takes into account the fact that the driving force of private capital flows in the economy is the pursuit of profit. Such a market-sensitive approach to influencing capital markets exists: it attempts to harness private investment to public purposes by creating economic incentives for financial intermediaries to channel funds in the right direction.

That a state government should use economic incentives to re-direct the flow of capital in part depends upon a view that capital market problems stem from the perversity of existing market incentives. For example, the interest rates charged by a commercial bank may not reflect the appropriate cost of borrowing because the lender is excessively risk averse. Or a multi-billion dollar insurance company may choose to make a small number of large loans at a low rate rather than a large number of small loans at a higher rate because the information on the larger deals is far more cheaply and easily available, and the costs of putting together the small deals is so high. Perverse market incentives interfere with access to capital. A venture subject to them will have less capital available to it than it should.

Making Capital Available to Viable, Underfunded Firms

The incentive to which financial intermediaries respond in allocating capital is, obviously, the rate of return a project (such as a manufacturing business or housing development) pays relative to the risk they must assume. Consequently, a state government wishing to direct more funds toward a particular class of projects must either make it easier for the venture to meet the return required by financial intermediaries or reduce the risk that financial intermediaries must assume in making such investments, or do both. To make it easier for projects to pay the required return, the state can offer interest subsidies. To reduce the risk suppliers of capital must assume in funding projects, the state can guarantee loans and investments. In addition, the state can support the information and transaction cost of financial deals; thus either reducing the return intermediaries demand from their debtors as compensation for these high costs, or increasing capital availability through increased information.

How do interest subsidies and guarantees work? In the case of interest subsidies, the state pays the difference between the rate of return that flawed capital markets demand of an enterprise and the rate that should be demanded in terms of public efficiency and equity objectives. The financial intermediary thereby receives the market rate of return, and the recipient of capital pays this rate less the subsidy. A greater number of enterprises will thus be able to afford to raise funds, and their demand for capital increases. The supply of funds should increase in response; how much increase there is in supply will depend, however, on the extent of credit rationing, where firms are willing to pay the higher price but go unsatisfied in their demand because risk-averse lenders would rather not lend than increase their risk and return.

An illustration of the relative importance of the cost of financing as opposed to its availability to small firms is the reaction to the decision by several large banks last winter to set aside a small portion of their funds—with which they would lower the prime rate for small business loans by one or two percent. This move was primarily in response to a fear that interest rate "guidelines" might be imposed by the federal government due to rapidly rising rates. The response from owners and managers of small businesses around the country was generally unenthusiastic. The typical comment, from the owner of a refrigerator company in Wisconsin, was, "The availability of capital is more of a concern to me than the cost" (Rout, 1979).

In the case of guarantees, the state pledges to cover any default on the part of the private borrower (or a portion of the default). This makes the financial risk zero (or less than it would be without any guarantee) for the financial intermediary. Borrowers backed by guarantees thus become more attractive to sources of capital, which in turn leads to a greater supply of capital to the borrowers in one of two ways. The guarantee may reduce the risk premium demanded by the intermediaries, thus increasing demand for funds in response to this lower interest rate and stimulating greater capital supply in response. Or the guarantee may mean that enterprises formerly subject to credit rationing will now receive capital as a consequence of the lower financial risk to the lender.

Guarantees are thus, in principle, a formidable tool for those economic policy makers concerned with increasing capital access. A big public policy issue, however, will be to ensure that scarce public resources only go to those risky enterprises that actually need the guarantee.

In increasing the availability of capital to small, young firms who have been unjustifiably denied funds, economic incentives can make a number of contributions. They can be used to mitigate excessive risk aversion, whether it is due to inefficient risk bearing or monopoly conditions in the credit market. A state guarantee can be especially effective in reducing the lender's risk to virtually nothing. The risk is shifted from the lender to the taxpayers of the state, who can bear it more efficiently. The state in turn charges the financed enterprise a fee for providing the guarantee and deposits this in a reserve fund established to pay off possible defaults. In essence, this fee represents a risk premium paid to the taxpayers of the state. Industrial mortgage insurance programs in a number of states serve this function quite efficiently.

Reducing risk to financial intermediaries through guarantees will also reduce their demand for information on borrowers. Thus, a source of barriers to capital for many firms will be minimized. Subsidies could also be used to reduce those information and transaction costs directly to the bank. As an alternative, a state agency could be set up to act as an information gathering and distributing service, doing what existing business credit rating services do but focusing on new and small enterprises. It could reduce information costs by achieving economies of scale in evaluating borrowers. These savings can be passed on to either lenders or borrowers.

Finally, by reducing information costs and introducing more efficient risk bearing, financial intermediaries will be less likely to use group characteristics, such as sex or race or organizational form, as a method of credit screening.

In actually designing and implementing an economic incentive program, the key decisions revolve around targeting—that is, determining eligibility for the program, setting the level of the incentive, delivering the incentive, and paying for its costs.

Defining eligibility is equivalent to determining which investment projects deserve a boost in private capital markets. It requires a serious review of reasons for intervention, to ensure that the key ingredient missing from the enterprise is access to capital. Eligibility should be established in such a way that only those enterprises suffering from market imperfection, or financial intermediaries causing it, can receive economic incentives. Otherwise, subsidies and guarantees will be squandered on firms for whom the cost and availability of capital is not a significant issue. Giving subsidies or guarantees to large firms which do not need them is a major hidden cost of any state subsidy or guarantee program. However, it must also be remembered that narrowing eligibility criteria has costs attached to it as well. Resources must be spent on researching and identifying firms eligible for assistance, and on administrative structures that will actually implement the eligibility requirement judiciously.

Deciding how much of a loan to guarantee or how large a subsidy to give is also an important step. Too high an incentive means wasteful expenditure; too low an incentive means falling short of the program objectives. Just as economic incentives set in the private market—prices—continuously re-adjust in response to changing conditions, state economic conditions will require experimentation, evaluation and modification as well.

Once a decision is made about eligibility and level of incentives, state policy makers must decide on the most effective method for delivering the incentive.

Finally, the subsidy or guarantee must be paid for.

Lowering Capital Costs to Attract Business Location

In practice, economic incentives have been generally used not for increasing *access* to capital for projects suffering from capital market imperfections, but for reducing the *cost* of capital in order to induce firms to start-up or expand in a state. Any state considering lowering capital costs as an incentive to stimulate economic activity should be aware of several very serious obstacles.

First, interstate and interregional market and production cost differences can be substantial. Any capital subsidies would have to be very large and quite expensive to compensate an enterprise for the higher labor, land, energy, transportation or other real production costs location in the state would entail. To cite one example, an interest subsidy that reduces the effective borrowing rate from 10 percent to 2.5 percent (a quite large subsidy in this country) would, on average, increase a firm's rate of profit by only 0.3 percent (Daniels and Kieschnick, 1979). It is unlikely that this change would be at all sufficient to offset unattractive market or production features in a state's economy. When studies on the efficacy of capital subsidies in the U.S. are reviewed, "the overwhelming consensus is that tax and fiscal concessions rarely have much effect on interstate and interregional choices of industrial location" (Cornia et al., 1978).

In Europe, where capital subsidies have been more effective, they average 25 percent of the total capital cost (principal plus interest) of *each* employee; in Canada the figure is 30 percent (Philip, 1978; Nathan, 1979). The depth of these subsidies is far beyond the bounds of practical politics in most American states. For this reason alone, it is likely that the offered subsidy is insufficient to make any difference, and thus is a waste of scarce taxpayer dollars.

Second, unless the state can predict very accurately the cases where a subsidy will make a difference, a lot of money will be wasted giving subsidies to firms that would have located or expanded in the state anyway. Traditionally, state and local governments have not done a good job of targeting subsidies. Highly paid corporate lawyers, accountants and managers of firms are much better at making an impressive case for a deep subsidy than state officials are at challenging it. In a typical case, an economic development official in one Midwestern state believed that a 12-year property tax abatement was necessary to lure a $20 million sodium bicarbonate plant to the state: "The tax incentive was the keystone of the deal." But a high official of the company admitted, "The tax abatement was a nice kicker at the end, but we chose the state mainly because of its strategic location for distribution and market growth" (Alsop, 1978). This example confirms our first two points: the subsidy was not necessary at all, and the state could not evaluate the depth of subsidy required.

Third, the above example also illustrates another point—in the absence of the ability to evaluate what subsidy is really called for (if any), the state is inclined to give the maximum allowed whether it is needed or not.

Fourth, although the subsidy is usually not enough to change a location decision, once having decided to relocate (or stay) in a particular place, few firms will refuse the subsidy. Since the subsidy makes no difference in the decision, it is merely a misuse of scarce resources.

Finally, subsidies that reduce the cost of capital will be worth the most to capital-intensive firms, when more labor-intensive firms may be desired for purposes of job creation. If a state wants to use economic incentives to attract investment, it would be better off subsidizing labor costs directly. As a general proposition, any subsidy should be *directly* targeted, rather than indirectly provided through interest subsidies or tax incentives. That way the true cost is clear, the subsidy is likely to be more efficiently applied, and the underlying feasibility of the venture is not obscured.

All of these criticisms concerning capital subsidies apply with equal force to the tax incentives analyzed in Chapter 2. Although the instruments are different, the impact is the same; neither can typically lower the cost of capital enough to change a location decision. Therefore, both are bad public policy.

DIRECT STATE FINANCIAL INTERMEDIATION

Both approaches to public credit allocation discussed so far make use of private financial intermediaries in channeling capital. Through either administrative regulation or economic incentives the state encourages these institutions to make investments that otherwise would not occur. While these two strategies have their advantages, public capital allocation can be accomplished in a more direct and often superior manner. Instead of channeling funds through its influence on private intermediaries, the state can operate its own public financial intermediary. In fact, thirty states and Puerto Rico have done just that. More than half of these institutions have been established since 1970, and as of 1974 had $14 billion in assets (Kimball, 1976).

How does a state financial intermediary work? In essence, the state either borrows in the capital market or taxes the wealth of its citizens to raise funds and then relends or invests them in projects it believes do not have adequate access to private financial institutions.

A state may also choose to employ state financial intermediaries to provide below market rate financing to businesses in an attempt to influence industrial location. However, all of the caveats raised about capital subsidiaries apply here. In addition to the five strong objections listed above, subsidies will require greater dependence of a state financial intermediary on legislative appropriations, a relationship which can cause the institution to be excessively erratic, political, or conservative in its financing. Dependence on annual appropriations will either lead the development bank to respond to the short-term political objectives of the legislature, or spend its money within the one or two year time frame of the appropriations, or be too careful about the soundness of the ventures it finances (thus becoming as risk averse as the private market). In any event, the agency will act more like a government bureaucracy and less like an independent development finance institution.

Making Capital Available to Viable, Underfunded Firms

The history of America's financial system includes a history of continual innovation by intermediaries that has improved capital market efficiency. State financial intermediaries can contribute to this innovative tradition by offering new and needed credit services for business enterprises, the housing market, and public infrastructure in support of economic development. Specifically, these institutions can help correct capital market imperfections by providing more efficient risk bearing, reducing information and transaction costs, promoting competition and alleviating discrimination.

First, they can offer opportunities for risk bearing not otherwise available in private capital markets. As outlined in Chapter 1, the precondition for risk pooling is the spreading of a risky investment among a sufficiently large number of individual portfolios so that each share will represent only a small fraction of each of those portfolios. In this way, the investment's non-systematic risk can be canceled out. To go into these individual portfolios, a risky investment must be divisible. When financed by a state financial intermediary, this divisibility can be achieved by a large number (thousands of households) of citizens in the state bearing the risk. These taxpayers run the risk of increased taxes or reduced services if the enterprise does poorly. In this manner a fraction of the risky enterprise becomes a component of their individual portfolios and is diversified. For larger enterprises that would normally be funded through a public capital market or through a large private financial intermediary, we would not expect that the state could bear the risk in a more efficient manner. But for the numerous new and young enterprises that are substantially financed by family and associates, a state financial intermediary has the opportunity to do a better job. This means that productive investments formerly put off because their risk was not sufficiently diversified by the capital market can now be made.

Second, the cost of information gathering in evaluating possible financings can be reduced by a state financial intermediary. To begin with, when risk is borne more efficiently, less information will likely be required to evaluate a venture. Moreover, the large number of small and young enterprises a state intermediary will deal with may produce economies of scale that reduce information costs per dollar of financing. This has proved true in the case of the $100 million Massachusetts Capital Resource Corporation. Even if information costs are not lowered, the financial institutions can charge a higher interest rate to compensate itself for these costs. By definition, these are more profitable, riskier firms that can afford to pay a risk premium in order to gain access to capital. Otherwise, they should not be financed. Banks and other private institutions may not do this, choosing to ration credit away from such risky investments instead of charging them a higher rate.

Third, the costs of financial transactions can be reduced. The cost of otherwise prohibitively expensive capital market transactions can be reduced by channeling a large volume of similar deals through a single, central state institution. This institution can both spread its overhead over a large number of these transactions and become highly skilled in packaging and servicing them. As in the case of information costs, even if transaction costs are not lowered, the financial intermediary can charge a higher interest rate to compensate itself for these costs. Again, banks and other private institutions may not do this, simply avoiding such transactions, as they often do.

Fourth, the state intermediary could increase competition in capital markets, including commercial banking markets. The impact of public financial institution entry on capital market structure and performance will depend on the particular segment of the market it operates in, its size, and the terms it offers.

Fifth, a state financial intermediary can pursue nondiscriminatory lending policies. By reducing information costs and introducing more effective risk bearing, the public intermediary will be less likely to use group characteristics, such as sex or race or organizational form, as a method of credit screening. By staffing the institution with personnel sensitive to discrimination, straightforward prejudice can be eliminated. One of the aims of the new state chartered Alaska Commercial Fishing and Agricultural Bank, which will be owned and operated by its users, is to eliminate the classic prejudice which banks have had against financing fishermen.

Funding a State Financial Intermediary A state financial institution can only operate as a capital-providing enterprise if it has a reliable source of funds. Moreover, only certain methods of funding the intermediary will be consistent with each of the capital-market correcting uses of funds just discussed. Three general sources of capital are worth consideration:

- issuing tax-exempt bonds;
- receiving a legislative appropriation from tax revenues;
- obtaining time and savings deposits of state and local agencies and private citizens, or investing state and local pension funds.

Each has its advantages and disadvantages. We will describe how each works, and then discuss how to choose among them.

Most state financial intermediaries raise funds by issuing tax-exempt bonds, whose market we described in Chapter 3. Using this method of financing for a state development bank is anything but straightforward. For the state must choose among different varieties of tax-exempt bonds, each variety having a different form of security pledged to back up its debt service payments in case of default. *General obligation bonds* of the state are backed by the full taxing power of the state government issuing them. *General obligations of a state agency* are backed by the revenues of the sponsoring agency, not by the state government as a whole. *Revenue bonds* have only the revenues of the project or business ultimately financed by money raised from the bond issue as security. Finally, so-called *moral obligation bonds* do not legally commit the state to cover defaults but "morally obligate" it to do so.

Constitutional limits on the total amount of different tax-exempt debt the state can have outstanding, or on the uses of general obligation financing, may constrain the choice of what bond-type to use. But to the extent a choice can be made, major trade-offs must be confronted.

On the one hand, bonds more strongly obligating the state to cover default offer greater benefits in some key ways. The backing of the taxing power of the state means a bond issue will command a higher credit rating than if only the assets and revenue of the enterprises ultimately using the capital are pledged as security. This results in lower borrowing costs for the issue. More importantly, revenue bonds (and, to a lesser degree, the general obligation bonds of a state agency) limit state intermediary lending to those enterprises which would be evaluated as a good credit risk by private financial institutions and investors. With revenue bonds, the risk of the bond is the risk of the final recipient of the funds raised. Investors will not purchase such bonds at all (or will charge very high interest premiums) without assurances that the proceeds will be used for relatively safe projects. This limitation could take the state right back to one of the very problems it set out to solve with the new intermediary—the failure of private capital sources to properly evaluate and finance certain kinds of enterprises. Although this means of financing has proved to be reasonably sound for state housing finance agencies financing multi-unit housing, to gain maximum freedom in the use of funds it raises, a state financial intermediary must substitute the perceived creditworthiness of the state for the creditworthiness of the ultimate users of funds. This implies moving toward the general obligation bond, or providing substantial security for revenue type bonds beyond actual project revenues, as some states have done.

On the other hand, bonds more strongly obligating the state to cover defaults entail greater costs in other ways. The greater the state guarantee, the greater will be the risk borne by the taxpayers of the state. This is an implicit cost, since the taxpayers are not in a position to demand compensation for bearing this risk. A greater degree of bonding obligation may adversely affect the state's overall credit rating—an explicit cost that will show up in the interest rates it pays across the board in future borrowings. Just as more highly leveraged businesses face a greater prospect of financial distress, so do more highly leveraged states and municipalities. And those who purchase their bonds will charge them accordingly, or not buy the bonds at all—exactly what happened to the New York Urban Development Corporation and New York City.

Debt financing through the bond market does not represent the only potential source of capital for a state financial intermediary. Another alternative source is tax revenue. Instead of borrowing on the collateral of the state's wealth (which happens in a bond issue), this wealth can be tapped directly through the state government's taxing power. For example, between 1958 and 1972 the Pennsylvania Industrial Development Authority received its funds for lending to firms in distressed areas through annual legislative appropriation. Again, there are pluses and minuses and tradeoffs. First, this method of raising funds may be very disruptive to the current operating expenditures of the state, even assuming that the loaned capital is fully recovered as the borrowing enterprises pay off interest and capital. If a tax on consumption, it does, however, guarantee that the state will not simply displace existing capital flows when it finances new enterprises. It also gives the intermediary freedom to depart from the judgment of the private investors to whom the firm would otherwise turn to for funds. On the other hand, annual appropriations from the legislature may introduce short-term political considerations into the decision-making process which are manifestly unsound from a long-range economic development standpoint. Finally, if the tax is not progressively structured—which many state taxes are not—this financing method may have undesirable distributional effects.

Another alternative is for the state intermediary to accept the deposits of private individuals and/or public agencies, just as a commercial bank would. The state-owned Bank of North Dakota, for instance, acquires funds in just this way. A potential problem with this source of funds is that the intermediary will experience substantial seasonal fluctuations in its deposit base since the accounts of its state and local agency customers will vary with their budgetary cycles. This may restrict the intermediary to loans and investments of relatively short maturities, and a level of risk no different from that of private banks.

The billions of dollars in state regulated public employees retirement systems, on the other hand, offer more creative opportunities for increasing returns to the benefited employees while improving the investment climate in the state. In Chapter 6, we will explore ways to do this which are true to the trustees' fiduciary responsibility.

When the state intermediary is involved in providing equity financing to projects, special problems regarding the sources of funds are raised. Income from its equity financings will ebb and flow, with the likelihood of no return at all in the early stages. Consequently, if the institution is funded through a general obligation bond issue, it will not always be able to pay the constant demand of interest and principal payments to the bondholders. Either debt service payments must be paid out of general state tax revenues, as is the case with the Massachusetts Community Development Finance Corporation (CDFC), or the entire capital of the development bank must come out of general state revenues, as is the case with the Alaska Renewable Resources Corporation (ARRC). An untried, but potentially suitable third source of long-term funds for an equity providing institution will be state retirement systems.

OPTIONS FOR FINANCING BUSINESS ENTERPRISE: INFLUENCING PRIVATE FINANCIAL MARKETS AND INSTITUTIONS

In applying the principles of Chapter 4 to workable solutions for correcting private capital market failures that adversely affect business enterprise, state policy makers have two major policy options: *first,* use state regulatory authority and economic incentives to redirect private capital flows, and *second,* create new state-controlled financial institutions intended to do what the private market would not. Both are realistic alternatives with different strengths and weaknesses. In this chapter, we will explore operating models of state efforts to influence the investment decisions of private financial institutions and investors. In Chapter 6, we will compare those policies to direct state intermediation in capital markets.

USING STATE REGULATORY AUTHORITY TO INFLUENCE PRIVATE CAPITAL FLOWS

Spurred by the recognition that regulatory authority might be used to combat geographic "redlining" in mortgage lending, a number of states have awakened to the potential of administrative regulation as a tool for re-directing private capital flows in support of business development. Historically, regulation of state-chartered private financial intermediaries has given short shrift to the objective of fostering state economic development. Not only has this concern been neglected as a specific objective, but the other goal of regulation—ensuring the safety of citizens' savings, preserving the profitability of the financial institution, and protecting against fraud and mismanagement—have often been pursued in ways which unnecessarily stifle state economic development. Thus, in reviewing regulation of financial intermediaries, a state government must consider, *first,* statutes and regulations that are primarily intended to shift capital to businesses which are crucial to development but are capital poor; and *second,* statutes and regulations primarily promulgated to achieve other objectives, but which secondarily either facilitate or inhibit such loans and investments. These two sets of issues arise in every area of regulation: Liability regulations affecting the sources of funds, asset regulations affecting the uses of funds, and market structure regulations authorizing the chartering of new institutions or the branching of existing institutions. We will consider each of these areas in order.

Regulating the Sources of Funds: Liabilities Although asset regulation would seem to be a much more direct way to affect who and what kinds of firms gain access to funds, in fact, liability regulation has a significant indirect impact. The reason is simple: *uses* of funds are constrained by *sources* of funds.

As we saw in Chapter 3, commercial banks which are largely dependent on short-term deposits are severely limited in their ability to provide small firms with the kind of long-term debt capital they need for expansion. Similarly, a major source of funds for SBICs and MESBICs—SBA debentures—limits those specialized kinds of venture capital companies in their ability to invest equity in young ventures; they must inexorably pay back SBA the fixed interest and principal on the debt, even if the firms they invest in cannot pay the venture capitalist. Moreover, as rising money market rates drive depositors out of price-regulated markets (such as thrift institutions) into unregulated markets, the ability of the thrifts to make housing loans is severely curtailed. Finally, as more and more financial resources become concentrated in fewer and fewer much larger financial intermediaries, the relatively high information and transaction costs of smaller loans will encourage these larger institutions to make a small number of large loans rather than a large number of small loans.

As a general proposition, loosening restrictions on the price, term and nature of liabilities will increase competition between classes of financial intermediaries and will tend to encourage them to look for more creative ways to lend or invest their assets.

In 1959, many analysts saw the commercial banks as going the way of the railroads. Numerous new financial markets were being innovated: commercial paper, household finance, equipment leasing and factoring. Each of these passed the banks by in much the same way as airplanes and trucking overtook the railroads. But Citibank's regulatory innovation of a new source of funds, the negotiated certificate of deposit, changed all that. Quite suddenly, commercial banks were no longer required to sit back and wait for depositors to come in the door. They could now go out and buy money when they needed it, with their own kind of commercial paper.

The implications of this were enormous for capital markets, and profoundly altered centers of power, rates of growth and uses of funds throughout the financial community. Bankers, who had become quite passive throughout the Depression and World War II, could now aggressively seek whole new fields of borrowers, confident that they could buy funds with C.D.s to cover demand. Commercial banks could now aggressively think of themselves as like "transportation" companies, not railroads, and find many new uses for funds because of this new source.

When New England thrift institutions challenged commercial banks with the regulatory change permitting N.O.W. accounts (negotiable orders of withdrawal); which are in effect interest bearing checking accounts, the impact was quite similar. Once sleepy savings banks aggressively took on commercial banks for daily deposits. But these new sources of funds increased their costs of doing business, in turn forcing the savings bankers to look for higher return (and higher risk) uses of funds. This led many savings bankers to move from a market they knew well, single-family housing loans, to higher risk and higher return long-term industrial and commercial mortgages—precisely the kind of long-term debt capital that expanding small firms need and can seldom get from commercial banks. Because the risks were higher and the field was not well known to them, they felt the need to push for the chartering of new institutions which could better pool and spread the higher risk, as well as pool new knowledge and create transaction cost efficiencies. Two such institutions are described below: a consortium of savings banks in western Massachusetts called New L.I.F.E. and the proposed Massachusetts Lending Corporation.

Finally, credit unions are the financial intermediary growing at the fastest rate—precisely because they are exempt from the price regulation ceiling of "regulation Q" which governs commercial banks and thrift institutions. These higher costs of doing business, in turn, are leading the more aggressive credit unions to seek higher return uses, as well as to push for regulatory changes that will permit them to lend in new and riskier markets such as commercial lending.

The opportunities available to state banking, thrift and insurance regulators to increase and direct the uses of assets by liberalizing and diversifying the sources of liabilities is an opportunity so far seldom seized. To date virtually all efforts at positive liability regulation have been directed toward holding a ceiling on the cost of deposited liabilities in order to keep down the cost of loaned assets. But we have seen that this constrains the availability of capital from regulated institutions in several ways: *first,* when unregulated intermediaries are willing to outbid regulated institutions for funds, the regulated ones have nothing to lend; *second,* a cap on the cost of liabilities discourages competition for those deposits and does not encourage the regulated institution to seek those higher risk loans that would cover the higher cost by providing a higher return. Creative liability regulation would remove barriers to competition on the liability side in order to encourage more aggressive risk taking on the asset side. In other words, it would directly improve the efficiency of capital markets in ways which would stimulate the flow of capital to those job-generating, young, small firms so crucial to state economic development.

Regulating the Use of Funds: Assets

Of all the possible ways to support business financing through state intervention in capital markets, the least activity has been in the regulation of asset holdings—what financial intermediaries loan to and invest in. This is not surprising, since mandating uses of funds counter to the normal practice of the regulated institutions would likely impose costs on them (or, often just as important, perceived costs). This, in turn, can provoke the kind of retaliation discussed in our introduction to asset regulation in the last chapter. A case in point: When the Texas legislature passed a law in 1902 requiring insurance companies in the state to invest a certain proportion of their premium income in Texas, twenty-nine companies—virtually every major out-of-state insurance firm operating in the state—withdrew immediately. The statute has since been rescinded, but the lesson lives. Thus, in a state like Illinois, such a mandatory investment law has been proposed in the legislature fourteen times this century. Despite broad support, it has never passed (Orren, 1974).

An alternative to mandating investments—what we have called the "carrot" approach to asset regulation—has not been widely used either. When state governments have chosen to give an *incentive* for a certain type of investment, they have typically chosen to use the tax system or provide an outright subsidy. The most likely regulatory incentive, as we noted in the previous chapter, would involve relaxing legal reserve requirements in exchange for particular kinds of loans on investments. In general, however, reserve requirements for state-chartered banks do not generally appear to really affect bank holdings of reserve-type assets. In almost all states, non-Federal Reserve member banks who are subject only to state regulation hold cash reserves substantially larger than those required by law (Gilbert, 1978). So relaxing this requirement will not really offer any incentive.

Changes in asset regulation which seem to have the most effect are those which relax existing constraints on lending to or investing in profitable enterprises. These firms need capital and would receive funds in ways which profit the banks if there were not legal barriers. A dramatic example of this approach is provided by Massachusetts, which recently found that its "legal list" only permitted its $30 billion thrift industry to invest in *one* multinational company headquartered in the state. No other investments in local manufacturing corporations were legal, despite the fact that the state's economy is largely dependent for jobs and tax base on the growth and expansion of young, small, profitable electronics firms.

Now, through a cooperative effort of the savings bankers association, the High Technology Business Council, the banking commission and the legislature's banking committee the legal list rules have been amended to make eligible all profitable manufacturing firms in the state with at least $25 million in sales.

As an alternative to across the board liberalization or elimination of legal lists, many states have opted for so-called "leeway" provisions. Under these exceptions (or "leeways") to legal lists, banks and thrift institutions can invest a small percent—less than 5 percent—of their assets in higher risk enterprises for the purposes of community and economic development. In some states, community development corporations are eligible, for example. Unfortunately, leeway provisions are commonly used to further the development of the thrift institutions themselves, rather than the community. For example, "leeway" investments are often used to construct new bank buildings. Careful targeting of the regulatory incentive could avoid such a misuse of scarce, high-risk resources.

We conclude this section as we began it: creative asset regulation, like its close companion, liability regulation, should be the cutting edge of new innovations in state development finance. Although the redlining issue has made policy makers aware of the possibilities of asset regulation for the first time, many of these initial efforts have been misguided in focusing almost exclusively on housing (see Chapter 7), rather than the provision of equity and long-term debt to younger, smaller commercial and industrial enterprises.

We suggest that there is an extraordinary opportunity for a new generation of policy-minded state banking and insurance commissioners to think more broadly and positively about the possibilities of *facilitating* the flow of state-chartered commercial bank, savings bank, cooperative bank, savings and loan, credit union and insurance company assets to profitable, growing firms within the state who are suffering from capital market imperfections.

Regulating Market Structure: Chartering New Private Financial Intermediaries

In exercising its authority to charter financial intermediaries, a state government acts as a gatekeeper for the supply side of capital markets. Beginning with the establishment of Business Development Corporations (BDCs) in the 1950s, there has been an awareness that this authority might be used to charter new, special purpose *private* financial institutions that would fill gaps in the existing institutional network. Then and now advocates of this approach argue that many of the capital market imperfections we have described could be eliminated by creating such intermediaries. They would finance small and other business enterprises unjustifiably denied credit by conventional lenders.

What promise does the chartering of new, development-oriented private intermediaries hold? How well have such institutions performed in the past and what are the prospects for the most current models? We will try to answer these questions by first examining the Business Development Corporation as it has emerged over the last two decades. Then we will move on to three interesting publicly chartered and privately capitalized models in Massachusetts—the NEW L.I.F.E. consortium, the proposed Massachusetts Lending Corporation, and the Massachusetts Capital Resources Corporation.

First chartered in Maine during 1949, about thirty states have Business Development Corporation enabling legislation on the books. Of these, twenty-seven now have active BDCs. There has been no growth in the number of BDCs in the past few years, their boom period having been in the 1950s and 1960s. The record of these institutions is mixed, with substantial variance among the states, but some general conclusions can be made.

BDCs were intended to lend to firms who had been refused credit by conventional lenders. These lenders would refer a marginal borrower to the BDC, and perhaps take a senior position in financing the firm behind the junior position taken by the BDC. For its sources of funds, a BDC typically starts out with $0.5 million to $2.0 million in equity raised through stock purchases by public utilities, commercial and industrial corporations, commercial banks and individual investors. It then borrows from commercial banks, savings banks and insurance companies on an unsecured basis, and lends out this money to businesses in the state. These sources of debt capital usually pledge a line of credit to the BDC for a number of years. The BDC usually borrows from them up to a debt/equity ratio of about 10 to 1.

It was originally thought that these institutions would be able to channel capital into businesses that conventional lenders would turn down—businesses that were risky but still offered a high enough expected return to offset this fact. Because of several unique characteristics, they would be able to do what existing intermediaries could not, and make a profit for their shareholders in the process. *First,* they could do things that other institutions were prevented from doing by federal or state regulation and monitoring, as well as traditional industry practice. For example, BDCs could make a loan to a borrower with insufficient collateral, or even on a completely unsecured or subordinate basis. *Second,* BDCs offered a greater opportunity for banks and other sources of funds to diversify the risk associated with small business loans. These institutions would, through their participation in the BDC, be getting a small piece of a lot of such loans. If, instead of investing in or loaning to the BDC, each institution took the equivalent of its stake and used it to directly finance the same type of risky business, it would have larger pieces of fewer such loans. These risky assets might not be as easily diversifiable in the institution's portfolio. *Third,* BDCs concentrated a particular type of loan in one intermediary, providing economies of scale that could reduce the often higher information and transaction costs associated with such smaller loans.

In terms of our analysis of how to correct capital market imperfections, these sound like well-designed institutions. But the performance of these special purpose, privately capitalized and operated intermediaries has fallen far short of their objectives, both in quantity and quality. Since their inception, BDCs have helped finance 3179 businesses. Five of these institutions have accounted for one-half this volume: Kansas, New Hampshire, Massachusetts, North Carolina and New York. In 1977, for example, there were only four new loans made per BDC, each averaging $246,000 (or a total of $1,100,000 in loans per BDC). Collectively, these institutions have a large unused borrowing capacity; they could almost double loans outstanding based on available lines of credit.

In the face of capital-deprived, credit-worthy firms, what can explain the failure of BDCs to fill the gap?

An easy answer might be that, in fact, there are no credit-worthy firms out there in the marketplace who have been denied capital. That is the answer often given by BDCs for their unused capacity and small portfolios. But one specific case study shows how this is not true. In its twenty-six-year history from 1953 to 1979, the Massachusetts Business Development Corporation has managed to accumulate a portfolio of $6,500,000. MBDC is, as we have noted, one of the more aggressive BDCs. In contrast, the Massachusetts Capital Resource Corporation, organized to finance the same high-risk small firms in Massachusetts, has developed a $32,000,000 portfolio in just eighteen months since it began operations in March 1978. How is it that these two institutions—organized to serve the same market in the same state, and along the same capital market perfecting lines of risk pooling, and information and transaction cost reduction—could have such radically different performance risks? The answers are instructive.

To begin with, BDCs are managed and supervised by individuals who have internalized the norms of conventional debt lenders. Their lending officers and board members generally come from other private debt financing institutions such as savings banks or commercial banks. These staffs have tended to be quite small—often one or two person shops—and they have tended not to be very aggressive in going out and finding appropriate loan opportunities. Also, the geographic concentration of BDC operations—they usually have only one office to cover a whole state—has often made it very expensive for them to research and negotiate loans on a statewide basis, especially with such small staffs.

Second, in terms of their uses of funds, they often lose the good loans that they make to the very conventional lenders who own and lend to the BDCs. This happens at two stages. A lot of borrowers withdraw their loan applications after they have been approved. Having been checked out by the BDC, the bank decides they are acceptable after all. Other borrowers pay off their BDC loans early on; having achieved some success they can re-finance themselves through a bank or other intermediary on better terms. In both cases, the BDC loses its income-producing loans early on and gets stuck with the "bad apples." Finally, member banks have a tendency to view BDCs as dumping grounds for failed loans that the bank no longer wants. Rather than aggressively using its funds to finance high-risk but profitable, growing, young firms, the BDC ends up as a bucket shop bailing out the dying ones.

Third, in terms of sources of funds, without question BDCs have been designed with and operated under far too high debt/equity ratios to finance high-risk, growing firms. They have been forced to avoid the riskier and potentially more profitable loans, let alone equity financings, because of the need for a strong, consistent cash flow to service their debt. But their equity shortage begs the question as an explanation for poor performance. In theory, a BDC could raise additional capital and reduce this ratio, as has the Rhode Island BDC (4 to 1). But they have generally not been able to pay significant dividends, and there is no market for their shares. Thus the equity shortage is more an effect than a cause of failure.

Legally, the broad and diverse ownership of BDCs—usually dozens of banks, thrifts and insurance companies spread across the state, represented by large and unwieldy boards—has made it difficult to determine who had a real stake in the success of the BDC, and who was in charge. One often is left with the impression that the BDC is a charitable organization run by volunteers who are seeking to do good, rather than an aggressive, innovative, and profitable market-correcting organization.

Within this general atmosphere of disappointing performance, a few successful BDCs stand out. Chief among these is the Kansas Development Credit Corporation. KDCC has been creative enough to stake out an area of operation far removed from traditional lending institutions in the state. It owns 51 percent of Kansas Venture Capital, Inc., an SBIC begun in 1977, and manages a "Kansas Funds Promote Kansas Jobs" program whereby KDCC buys SBA guaranteed loan participations from banks in the state and resells them to the state public employee pension funds, and other Kansas investors. No obvious structural characteristic built into KDCC can explain its aggressiveness. Certainly it has operated with high debt/equity ratios, just like the more conservative BDCs.

Caution must be exercised in interpreting the failure of the Business Development Corporations to have significant impact on capital market imperfections. Clearly, existing financial intermediaries and investors do need and desire new institutional vehicles for making certain kinds of transactions: that is, to do the very things that BDCs might have done in offering better risk pooling opportunities, reducing information and transaction costs, and having more flexible regulatory supervision.

The Massachusetts Capital Resource Corporation (MCRC) is just such a case in point (Gleisser, et al., 1979). In contrast to the Massachusetts Business Development Corporation, it has a highly paid seven-person professional staff drawn not from secured lending experience, but primarily from high-risk equity and venture capital financing of rapidly growing, small, high-technology firms. Its $100 million in capital is invested solely as equity by its partner Massachusetts insurance companies. Thus, it can be used to reinvest in fast growing, young firms as equity or subordinated debt. Its ownership and board are tightly concentrated in the five largest insurance companies in the state who know exactly why they must pursue a thoroughly professional aggressive investment program. If they do not invest $20 million per year for five years in MCRC, and if MCRC does not reinvest the bulk of those resources in rapidly growing, high-risk firms which generate a substantial number of new jobs in the state, then the insurance companies (who are taxed five times higher than the U.S. state average, and three times higher than the next closest state) will not get an agreed upon tax reduction. In other words, MCRC is serious business to both the state and the insurance companies, and is run that way. (For a discussion of some of its problems, see Ransom, 1979.)

A related case in point is the New L.I.F.E. (Low Interest For Expansion) Consortium in western Massachusetts (Day, et al., 1979). New L.I.F.E. is a group of twenty savings banks under the leadership of a seven-member steering committee. Non-statutory and subject to no special regulation, the Consortium makes mortgage loans to firms who are having trouble getting long-term money but nonetheless can under the right conditions offer a competitive return. No formal, written guidelines govern its operations. In practice, where a loan opportunity facing one of its member banks is too large and/or too risky, it refers the loan application to the Consortium, where the firm is reviewed by the steering committee. If the loan gets approved, then the originating bank becomes the lender, supplying the biggest chunk of money, with the remainder split among other member banks according to their size, geographic proximity to the borrower, and risk attitudes. Thus, the Consortium provides both risk pooling advantages and the information cost advantages inherent in a decentralized network of lending institutions, each serving the borrowers closest to them. In the words of the Consortium's steering committee chairperson, ". . . there was a capital gap in Springfield and New L.I.F.E. filled it."

In essence, New L.I.F.E. is an elaborate system for inter-bank loan participation. The concept is an old one, and in this case works quite well. One acknowledged problem the Consortium has encountered, however, suggests the advantges of either a more structured, special-purpose private institution or a public intermediary. According to a member banker, "New L.I.F.E. has some minor problems, most of which have to do with facilitating and expediting its operation. Any application entails getting information to and approval from a number of bank presidents and boards of investment. Occasionally, this can be a slow process. The cost of servicing a mortgage for a dozen or more banks can be burdensome."

That a state government can do something to facilitate programs like New L.I.F.E. on a statewide basis is the key premise in efforts to charter new, development-oriented, private financial institutions. In New L.I.F.E.'s home state, it has inspired the proposed Massachusetts Lending Corporation. Commercial banks, savings banks, cooperative banks, savings and loans, and credit unions may all become members of MLC, the only requirement being that they purchase stock in the institution. Each member must then make a loan commitment to MLC that cannot be revoked for five years. It will have a professional staff to process and package loans. There has been some resistance in the state's financial community to MLC, much of it surrounding the fact that member institutions will be participating in loans far removed from their local communities. This is more crucial than it might first appear to be. In supplying funds to smaller, riskier firms—the prime clients of an MLC—financial institutions often need the added, indirect incentive of increased business activity in their market area that the loan would produce, even though the borrowing firms offer direct financial benefits sufficient to merit financing in a well-functioning capital market. Moes (1962) argued that a geographic scope of operation too extensive for stockholders to capture these indirect benefits was at the root of BDC problems. And the exception that proves this rule would be the substate New L.I.F.E.

For this reason, Pennsylvania chartered three regional BDCs—one for metropolitan Philadelphia, one for greater Pittsburgh, and one for the rest of the state. And California's new variation on the old BDC theme, Business Industrial Development Corporations (BIDCOs) recognizes the problem by allowing BIDCOs to be chartered anywhere—even in competition with each other.

In summary, both MCRC and New L.I.F.E. suggest that more is at issue than structure in chartering new private financial institutions. The participating private financial institutions must have a genuine stake in whether or not the new institution works, if it is to work.

Regulating Market Structure: Branching of Private Institutions

While restrictions on where a bank may branch within its state supposedly protect the public, they in fact contribute substantially to monopoly and oligopoly banking market conditions that restrict the availability of credit, particularly to smaller enterprises. In thirty states banks are prohibited from setting up branch offices outside their home office counties (CSBS, 1977). Without question, this restricts the degree of competition in local banking markets. Many of the states with liberalized branching laws did not always have such a liberal policy, and had the same kind of non-competitive banking markets found in limited branching states. Comparisons of bank behavior before and after branch banks enter into their market area, referred to in Chapter 3, show that the fruits of branching liberalization include a larger proportion of deposits channeled into loans, a larger proportion of loans going to businesses, lower interest rates for borrowers, and improved service to customers.

Statewide branching is supported by the majority of independent commissions and banking analysts who have studied the issue. In 1971 a major opinion rendered by the Department of Justice to the Council of State Governments recommended that states liberalize their branching laws to deal with anti-competitive forces in commercial banking. That same year, the President's Commission on Financial Structure and Regulation (the Hunt Commission) recommended that "by state laws, the power of commercial banks to branch, both *de novo* (new banks) and by merger, be extended to a statewide basis, and that all statutory restrictions on branch or home office location based on geographic or population factors or on proximity to other banks or branches thereof be eliminated."

In spite of this support for statewide branching, and its record of success in many states, it has been criticized and resisted by some, including many state bank supervisors and commercial bankers. They argue that statewide branching leads to "overbanking": too many banks in a market area, endangering the solvency of the banking system. Moreover, it is argued that it may actually lead to less competition because the many small rural and town banks cannot survive against the fewer large urban banks. And it is argued that statewide branching will lead to a greater export of capital out of the local community, since banks based far away will be more prone and able to invest in other places. While each of these negative effects must be considered in formulating a branching policy, the evidence suggests they will be relatively minimal or non-existent.

To begin with, consider the "overbanking" argument. This term arose after the run of bank failures in the late 1920s and 1930s to describe what some thought was a market with too many (and consequently financially weak) commercial banks. In response to this perceived problem, several states and the federal government tightened requirements for bank formation and branching. Yet more detailed, retrospective analyses of the great wave of bank failures in the Great Depression shows this crisis arose primarily from a too restrictive monetary policy on the part of the Federal Reserve, which reduced bank liquidity and produced large losses in capital, and only in small part from the proliferation of banks at that time (Gambs, 1977; Benston, 1973).

Post-war experience with statewide branching in several states has provided direct evidence that "overbanking" with its consequent bank failures is more myth than fact. In these states there have been very few bank failures, and those can be attributed to embezzlement and poor management. Even if a bank were to fail as a result of competition from new branch banks coming into its county, the negative consequences would be limited. The existence of the Federal Deposit Insurance Corporation, to which virtually every bank subscribes, completely protects most depositors and prevents bank runs. And as long as there are other banks in the community or branching from outside is permitted, failure will mainly be an inconvenience. When the U.S. National Bank of San Diego went under in 1973, a combined announcement was made of its failure and of the acquisition of its branches and deposits by Crocker National Bank. In other words, U.S. National customers were now Crocker customers.

A corollary of the myth of overbanking is the myth of predatory competition by large urban banks when allowed to branch into small local market areas of small rural banks. While economies of scale in banking do exist—as banks get larger they can perform banking functions more cheaply—they are not as large as commonly thought, and are being continually eroded through the use of computer technology by even the smaller banks. That local banks can compete with large metropolitan bank branches has been borne out in the experience of several states, including California with its huge Bank of America and Wells Fargo Bank. Even if a community can only support one locally based bank, it could easily absorb one or more branch offices into the local banking market. In fact, a study in the early 1960s found that the number of banks active in non-metropolitan areas of a state increases with greater branching liberalization (Horvitz and Shull, 1964). While large banks may present certain evils, they also have the ability to increase effective competition in heretofore isolated banking markets.

One of the possible disadvantages associated with the entrance of an outside bank into a distant community, often noted by critics, is that they will export savings out of that community. After all, larger banks imply increased activity in regional and national capital markets. Their staff, size and image are geared to a large market area. Moreover, in contrast, the small, local bank will be prompted by its local ties and dependence to make loans that "outsider" banks will pass by. Do these arguments hold up? In fact, there may be counties in which good loan opportunities do not exist, but the bank is lending anyway because of community ties or inability to take advantage of more profitable opportunities elsewhere. Such counties could suffer a greater export of savings under statewide branching. But they will be very much in the minority. First, we have looked at evidence showing that even credit-worthy borrowers are sometimes refused by these local-based banks, casting doubt on their propensity to make marginal loans. Second, in looking at the loan-deposit ratios of monopoly and oligopoly market local banks, we can see that these institutions themselves can export a substantial amount of savings through net inter-bank sales of federal funds and net purchases of government securities, loan participations and certificates of deposit in outside banks. In fact, places (like Chicago) where redlining is believed to be prevalent are almost always in states with very restrictive branching laws. If the capital export tendency generally holds true, we would expect a reduction of bank loans in a community when a local bank is taken over through merger with an outside one. Two studies have found no evidence of this happening (Kohn, 1964; Horvitz and Shull, 1964).

We do not want to suggest that existing banks in oligopolistic markets will emerge unscathed from a move to statewide branching. Far from it, they will lose monopoly profits, in the form of both a reduced rate of return and/or greater risk. Not surprisingly, they have been the most vociferous opponents of such a policy. But actual bank failure will be the exception. To the extent that any banks do go under, which is a possibility in the case of the very smallest ones, the words of former Congressman Wright Patman should be kept in mind: "When we boast of no bank failures, let's remember that several other business firms may have failed because the banks did not take as many risks as they might have." In other words, a state must balance any concern it has for preserving the health of existing banks with concern for the welfare of the larger number of bank borrowers.

USING ECONOMIC INCENTIVES TO INFLUENCE PRIVATE CAPITAL FLOWS: SUBSIDIES AND GUARANTEES

In both promotional and academic literature on state business finance programs, capital subsidies and loan guarantees are often lumped together as "financial incentives"; little distinction is made between them. Actually they should be, and often are, fundamentally different in the way they influence state economic development. Capital subsidies are intended to change the investment location behavior of business corporations. Gurantees are intended to influence the lending behavior of banks and other financial institutions. Subsidies work by affecting the relative cost of capital. Guarantees work by affecting the relative availability of capital. Subsidies are meant to draw jobs that would have been in other states. Guarantees are not necessarily supposed to draw jobs away in any direct fashion (though this may be one of their effects) and can actually create truly new jobs. Capital subsidies are relatively expensive. Guarantees can cost a state virtually nothing. Subsidies typically are delivered through poorly targeted tax expenditures. Guarantees are delivered through more sensitive administrative means.

Understanding the differences between these two types of capital market related programs means acknowledging two contrasting approaches to the role of capital in state economic development policy. Themes which appear in evaluating these two programs re-emerge in any discussion of the basic principles that should underlie a sound development policy.

Subsidizing the Cost of Capital

In South Carolina, they call them "sanctuaries to protect profits." This figurative language describes the host of state programs intended to raise the profitability of business enterprise higher than it would otherwise be. This enhanced profitability represents an incentive that is to keep existing corporations in the state and bring new ones in from outside.

The major approach taken to raise profitability has been reducing the effective *cost of capital* to firms operating in the state. This raises the net, after-tax income to these corporations and thus their profitability. State programs designed to lower the cost of capital to participating firms have rapidly proliferated in recent years. Their popularity reflects the belief that the major source of employment growth in a state will be jobs for which it must actively compete with other states. It is further assumed that what state these firms choose to invest in will be influenced by capital subsidy programs.

This thinking has made capital subsidy programs a major weapon in the "War Between the States" over industrial location. The weapon has two variants. One involves giving businesses tax deductions or credits equivalent to some portion of their new capital costs for plant and equipment. In effect this lowers the cost of the firm's investment and raises its profits. The other variant involves offering companies loans at a subsidized or below-market rate. This second approach will be discussed in more detail in Chapter 6 when we examine the state financial intermediaries through which interest subsidies are delivered. Here we will focus on the tax subsidy of capital costs, although in reading this discussion of tax incentives, it should be kept in mind that most of the criticisms apply equally well to interest subsidies.

When the state of New Jersey ended its nine-year experiment with tax exemptions for capital expenditures by businesses in the year 1800, the twentieth century popularity of such programs was certainly not envisioned. Currently, twenty-one states exempt part of corporate income from the business income tax. Twenty-two states exempt or delay property tax payments on new land and buildings, and twenty-eight exempt or delay such payments on new capital equipment. In the case of property tax abatements, the state legislature gives localities the option of granting or not granting them to specific firms. Approximately half a dozen states grant tax credits for new or expanded manufacturing facilities. An investment tax credit allows a business to credit against its tax liability a certain percentage of the cost of investment. It is roughly equivalent to a grant covering that percent of capital costs (principal plus interest). The largest tax credit is 3 percent in Massachusetts. In fact, when then Governor Wilson ran against Congressman Carey in 1974, one of his principal campaign promises was to raise New York's 1 percent tax credit to equal Massachusetts. The reason: to stop Massachusetts from stealing New York firms!

Despite their prevalence, the benefits of these programs are quite limited. To begin with, the target of these programs is not as large as *commonly* believed. Wholesale relocations, which tend to get the most press and public attention, are rare: only 554 of the 140,093 manufacturing firms with over twenty employees did so between 1969 and 1976—less than one half of one percent of all new jobs created. New branch plants and new subsidiary establishments account for about 30 percent of new jobs created nationwide. Branch plant expansions and subsidiary establishment expansions account for about 20 percent of new jobs created nationwide. But even these figures overstate the number of "footloose" jobs, since the majority of jobs generated by branch plants and subsidiaries tend to have their headquarters or parent firms in the same region; and many are in the same state (Birch, 1979).

The investment location decision of these firms will be relatively insensitive to any changes in their state business tax burden. The lack of importance of such tax differences was explained in Chapter 2. To reiterate the argument stated there, the combination of the small share of state taxes in total production costs, their deductability from the federal income tax and the comparatively large differences in other production expenses and market proximities between states limit the effect of even outright forgiveness of these taxes.

While the benefits will be small, the cost of capital subsidies provided by tax exemptions and credits are not. Since many of the tax breaks are automatic and elected at the choice of the tax avoider—there does not even have to be the weakest evidence that the firm is investing because of the incentive—they accrue to virtually all of the firms building a new plant or adding capital equipment in the state. And even where the authorities have some discretion about granting an abatement, there is no way of knowing whether it is really necessary or not. Faced with the prospect of a major industry saying that it invested in A instead of B because of differences in tax breaks, public officials tend to be liberal in giving them out. Current tax losses from such programs in states like Michigan and Massachusetts have been estimated to be as high as $100 million annually.

In short, states seem to be paying out a substantial amount in the form of lost tax revenues and receiving very little economic development in return. Yet these programs have doubled in the past decade. At least two facts explain this trend. In part it reflects the success of business interests in convincing state governments that the capital subsidies do matter. The subsidies do lie in the interest of these firms whether they really affect their investment decisions or not. As the Planning Director of Cleveland, Ohio, Ed Waxman, put it, "Tax abatement rewards developers for going ahead and doing what they would have done anyway. It's the cherry on top of the chocolate sundae." A study of the policy-making process in Connecticut and Massachusetts (Harrison, 1976) showed that corporations seeking these "cherries" were crucial in establishing the tax incentives.

But beyond the explicit and implicit business lobbying, the availability of subsidies can *sometimes* actually determine where a firm locates or expands. This will be true when a corporation is choosing between two or more states that are identical with respect to basic production costs and market proximity. The classic case was the competition between Pennsylvania and Ohio for Volkswagen's North American plant that was to employ 5,000 workers. Pennsylvania won, but had to offer a lot of inducements in the process: $40 million to buy and refurbish an old Chrysler plant that was leased back to VW for 30 years, the first twenty at 1.75 percent interest; $25 million in low-interest revenue bonds; $6 million in loans from public employee pension funds; and a 95 percent foregoing of the company's local taxes for the first two years and 50 percent for the following three years.

The VW case illustrates both positive and negative lessons. On the one hand, unlike most instances where capital subsidies are given out, some evidence existed that such an incentive might cause a firm to locate in the state when it otherwise would not. On the other hand, there was little attempt to determine if the jobs were worth the massive subsidies that Pennsylvania had to offer up (ACIR, 1979).

To sharpen our understanding of this problem, the recent decision of Goodyear to build a $180 million radial tire plant in Lawton, Oklahoma is instructive. First, Goodyear decided to locate this new plant, the world's most technologically advanced tire plant, close to markets. The greatest market need for new production capacity was west of the Mississippi and east of the Rockies. Then Goodyear looked for adequate labor markets for 1400 employees and land for a plant nine football fields long. It found a handful of sites which would do. Only then did Goodyear indicate its intentions to the local and state governments of the possible sites. In effect, each was given a chance to bid to "put the cherry on top," but, in fact, from a market and production standpoint any would have been appropriate. In conclusion, it should be noted that the prize these communities were competing for was a highly automated, capital intensive plant costing $118,000 per job—a far cry from the more labor intensive small firms that produce half of all new jobs in our society, and really often do need capital.

In addition to their role in influencing investment *location*, many advocates of capital subsidies believe they increase the total *amount* of investment in the economy. It is argued that firms compare the profitability of investment at the margin with the cost of capital. If the cost of capital is lowered, investments at the margin become economic. But there are problems with this analysis when taken as a justification for capital subsidies.

First, at the individual firm level, there can be big jumps downward in the profitability of investment at the margin. Second, total investment in an economy cannot increase unless the total amount of savings also rises. So capital subsidies would have to be large enough to both bridge the profitability gap to marginal investment projects, and increase the return for savers sufficient enough to stimulate additional saving. Empirical studies of the federal investment tax credit, currently at 10 percent, have cast doubt on its ability to increase the total amount of investment in the economy, precisely because of these issues (Gravelle and Kiefer, 1979). By implication these studies call into question equivalent state capital subsidies pursuing a similar goal.

In light of these examples and the past experience of capital subsidy programs, should states continue to utilize these tools? Not in their present form, we believe. However, the fact that instances do exist where a state government is truly in competition with neighboring, nearly economically identical states for investment, means they cannot be abandoned entirely. Rather, they should be strictly circumscribed so that:

■ Subsidies can only be given where strong evidence can be presented that the investment will not be made otherwise.
■ Subsidies are kept proportionate to job and income benefits that the state would receive and do not overshadow them.
■ Full public disclosure of subsidies and offsetting benefits.

We know of no state which has such a restrained and well-targeted program. Nor do we know of any states that have carefully evaluated the costs and benefits. A recent study of five states that appear to have tried to target more carefully than others indicates none has adequately measured the impact of its incentives (Daniels and Pfifferling, 1978).

In the absence of such analysis, measurement and targeting, our advice is not to waste scarce state tax resources on either tax incentives or interest subsidies.

Guaranteeing the Availability of Capital In contrast to capital subsidies, state loan guarantee programs represent a promising but fairly undeveloped capital market policy for state economic development. Their promise lies in their capacity to help nurture certain business opportunities in a state's economy that private financial institutions have not taken advantage of for a variety of reasons. Thus, they try to build on unrecognized strengths in the existing state economy (rather than compensate for unattractive economic features by subsidizing capital costs of private corporations). Currently, thirteen states offer loan guarantees for plant construction and fifteen for equipment and machinery financing. This represents a substantial growth in the prevalence of these programs during the early 1970s.

Guarantees help reallocate capital in favor of small and medium-sized enterprises that have faced unjustified obstacles in acquiring funds. The reasons this type of viable yet capital-poor firm can exist in what many believe to be generally efficient capital markets were described in Chapter 3.

Shifting investment toward these businesses can produce job and income gains in one of two ways. If the funds ultimately come at the expense of other in-state businesses, then the gain will be the *difference* between what these firms could provide and what the equally or more productive newly financed firm can offer. If the funds ultimately come at the expense of out-of-state corporations, then the gain is the *total* employment and income of the newly financed firm. Thus the most effective guarantee programs will be those that best target to relatively productive but capital-poor enterprises in providing guarantees and then ultimately redirect private funds that would otherwise go to out-of-state firms.

State governments have used a variety of mechanisms to ensure that firms really needing the guarantees are in fact the ones receiving them. First, there are statutory or administrative eligibility requirements. For example, in New Jersey the borrower must show that it could not obtain conventional financing. But in other states, like Connecticut, the major factor that restricts guarantees to the capital-starved companies is the ceiling on the amount that the state can guarantee on a single loan. In Connecticut this figure is $10 million for a plant construction project and $5 million for capital equipment expansion. In Ohio the ceiling stands at $5 million. These limits are not so low, however, that they necessarily exclude the branch operations of large, credit-worthy national firms who do not really need the program.

The other filtering mechanisms consist of the various fees a firm must pay to use the program and receive a guarantee. For a $1 million loan guarantee in Connecticut, for example, the borrower must pay a $1,000 fee when applying and a $3000 fee once the guarantee is committed. More important, the firm pays an annual premium to the state on the outstanding balance of the loan as compensation for the state bearing the risk of the borrower's possible default. This fee usually amounts to 1/2 percent on a plant loan and 1 percent on an equipment loan. However, if the sum of these fees and premiums is less than what a financial institution would normally charge for its information, transaction and risk-bearing costs, then the non-handicapped firm will still have an incentive to use the guarantee program rather than simply going for a straight loan or mortgage.

Charging participating firms the full cost of the guarantee also helps screen out those enterprises that are so marginal that they could not survive without subsidized financing. This is the type of company that the guarantee program needs to exclude if its operations are *not* to result in taking money from the most productive and giving it to the least productive. The other "screening out" process comes at the stage where the private lender decides whether to make the guaranteed loan. Virtually all state loan guarantee programs now only guarantee 90 percent or less of a loan. This is so the private lender retains an incentive to effectively refuse those firms who do not present a reasonable probability of payback. A program in Vermont lost $4 million in bad loans when it was offering 100 percent guarantees!

To the extent that state loan guarantee programs have erred in granting guarantees, they have heavily erred to the side of caution. When four of five New England guarantee programs were surveyed in 1976, it was found that their loss rate was extremely low—only .5 percent to 1.5 percent. The Connecticut Industrial Mortgage Insurance (IMI) program states that, "Reasonable assurance of ability to pay the mortgage is of *primary* importance. *Also* considered are such factors as a project's contribution to the economy of the community and the state, and its impact on employment and tax revenues [emphasis ours]." Only 3 of 123 loans guaranteed by IMI have resulted in default.

Getting guarantees to those firms which if adequately financed can make a positive difference in state economic growth is only half the story. As we have outlined already, the other half is taking the reallocated funds from corporations who are making the least contribution (in the extreme, those from outside the state). We have found little awareness of this dimension of guarantee program design. This largely reflects the fact that the program administrators must consider displacement effects on a case by case basis. It will depend upon the specific circumstances of the bank making the guaranteed loan. Consider the following two examples.

The First National Bank is a large urban bank in a competitive market. It has the largest possible proportion of its assets already in loans, given its need for liquidity and adherence to legal reserve requirements. It would not give General Furniture Manufacturers a loan because the firm is a small, minority-owned company, and the bank believes that, given its lack of experience in dealing with such firms, the information and transaction costs in reviewing and monitoring the loan would be prohibitive. But with a commitment from the state to cover any future defaults by General Furniture, the bank feels it can make the loan. Given that the bank cannot put any more of its funds into loans, the money to make this loan will not come from selling off a national corporation's bond it owns or a government security. Rather, the funds will come from not making some other business or consumer loan to a local firm or household.

The Merchants and Planters Bank, on the other hand, is a smaller, rural bank that has a monopoly on lending in its area. Consequently it has been able to afford putting a relatively large proportion of its funds not into loans, but into less risky corporate bonds and government securities. United Canning Company, a small, young and relatively risky firm, has been unable to get a loan from the bank because of the lender's ability to earn a monopoly profit on the less riskier loans it makes, allowing it to forego the normally more profitable opportunity like United Canning. However, the bank will make the loan if the state guarantees it since it then becomes a relatively riskless alternative for the bank's funds.

Since Merchants and Planters is not "loaned-up," capital for this new loan will not come at the expense of some other local loan but from a reduction in holdings of securities from outside the state.

In general, we can say that guarantee programs will have their greatest marginal impact on employment growth in a state when they are extracting loans from *such* banks with abnormally large portions of their assets in corporate bonds and government securities.

What general lessons can state policy makers draw from the nature and experience of loan guarantee programs?

■ Establish eligibility criteria and administrative procedures that *effectively restrict loan guarantees* to firms where they will really make a difference. This may include requiring various evidence of inability to acquire capital from conventional sources.

■ Set fees and premiums to *reflect the true costs* of providing the guarantee. This will help screen out both too healthy and too weak candidates. Most existing programs do not do this; they charge fixed amounts or fixed percentages of loan principle. Thus there is no attempt to charge higher premiums for the riskier guarantee. (The Ohio Development Finance Corporation does have a more variable rate tied to the interest rate charged by the private lender, which itself will reflect some risk considerations.)

■ Leave a sufficient percentage of the loan unguaranteed to provide an incentive to the lender to screen and monitor effectively.

■ Consider granting lines of guarantee authority to banks in the state. This would allow them to apply a state guarantee up to some predetermined total dollar amount of loans and up to some percentage of any single loan. The advantage to this approach is that the agent dispersing the guarantees, the bank, has an incentive to apply the guarantee authority on those loans where it will make the most difference, as well as having the information needed to do this. Perhaps this can increase the application of guarantees beyond their limited numbers today; the largest program, in Connecticut, has guaranteed only about ten loans per year since 1961.

If designed and implemented properly, loan guarantee programs can be a very cost-effective job-creation tool. The revenues of the program cover all of its expenses. A good program will serve a firm like our United Canning example, which, without the guarantee provided to it, would have been unable to expand its business. A less than perfect one will serve firms like Haas Food Manufacturing, the Austrian multinational that makes PEZ candies and dispensers, who received a loan guarantee from the Connecticut Development Authority when it set up a branch plant in the state.

6

OPTIONS FOR FINANCING BUSINESS ENTERPRISE: CREATING STATE-OWNED FINANCIAL INTERMEDIARIES

In contrast to state business finance strategies which seek to influence the flow of private capital through regulations and incentives—an old field wanting for new ideas—the creation of state-owned development finance intermediaries is a young field full of innovation. Although, as we indicated in Chapter 5, there are lots of creative options for liability and asset regulation to reduce capital market imperfections, so far few good models have been put into operation. Since 1970, however, there has been an explosion of new kinds of state owned financial intermediaries. Although some of these—such as the equity financing institutions—are too new to have a measurable track record, all are subject to review from the standpoint of the conceptual framework we established in Chapter 4. Some, such as tax-exempt bond financing intermediaries, are old enough to be soundly critiqued.

For purposes of this analysis, we can group these state development finance institutions into four categories: tax-exempt bond-financed, debt intermediaries, the largest and generally least effective group; contrasting tax-financed debt intermediaries; an interesting new generation of state-owned equity financing institutions; and, finally, an until recently overlooked group of public intermediaries with a fiduciary responsibility to pension holders, taxpayers or depositors, such as public employee retirement systems, the Western State Natural Resource Funds, or the State Bank of North Dakota.

DEBT INTERMEDIARIES FINANCED THROUGH BONDS

In state development finance, the giants have feet of clay. State authorities which sell tax-exempt bonds to finance business enterprise raise amounts of capital far eclipsing any other kind of state financial intermediary. But this huge volume of financing obscures their general impotence and irrelevance. It is important to understand why they are ineffective and how they can be bolstered or replaced.

When one speaks of bond-financed debt intermediaries, two different types of tax-exempt programs are being grouped together: one using revenue bonds and the other, general obligation bonds.

Revenue bonds are distinguished from general obligation bonds by the more limited security backing them up.

In the case of revenue bonds, a state or locality issues tax-exempt bonds to finance the plant and equipment for a specific corporation. This plant or equipment is then leased or sold on installment to the firm. Principal and interest on the bonds must be paid *exclusively* out of these lease or installment payments.

In contrast, debt service payments on general obligation bonds can and must be paid out of the general revenues of the issuing state or local jurisdiction if necessary.

Forty-eight states allow revenue bond financing of industry; forty-five of these states also authorize their municipal and county governments to issue them as well. Fourteen states authorize general obligation financing of industry.

It is the more popular industrial *revenue* bond (IRB) that has been the object of well-deserved wrath; the industrial *general obligation* (g.o.) bond-financed intermediaries (or bond insurance programs that mimic them) possess greater promise and will be examined after we analyze industrial revenue bond programs, or "IRB" programs, as they are popularly called.

Critiquing Tax Exempt Industrial Revenue Bonds

The near universality of IRB programs grows out of the same assumptions and pressures that have made tax incentives so popular despite ineffectiveness. For IRB financing is merely a vehicle for subsidizing the cost of capital—a subsidy that is seldom effective, whether in the form of tax incentives or interest reductions.

This particular capital subsidy comes in the form of an interest rate differential between the taxable debt instruments that a private firm would typically issue, and the federally tax-exempt bonds that Congress permits state and local governments to sell. Buyers of these tax-exempt bonds accept a lower pre-tax rate of interest, since their interest income will not be taxed by the federal government—thus yielding at least an equivalent post-tax rate of interest. This means an interest savings accrues to the IRB issuing authority which, in turn, is passed on to the company whose facilities are financed. This capital subsidy is perceived as useful in attracting investment by out-of-state companies or retaining in-state firms and entrepreneurs considering investing somewhere else.

IRBs have all the appeal of a free lunch. The subsidy comes from the federal government which gives up its tax revenue, permitting the lower interest costs. Yet like many free lunches, they have little nutritional value for the state sponsoring them. The reduced costs of production these capital subsidies provide to the beneficiary corporations are in the same range as the investment-related tax concessions previously outlined. In other words, they do not amount to much in light of total production costs or market differences among states, even in a region with similar production costs among the states. IRBs have been found (in a recent comprehensive review of the evidence) to be "at best of marginal, but not critical, value as an inducement to location in a state within a given region." (IILED, 1979.)

In about two-thirds of all IRB financings, the interest subsidy does not matter at all. Only in a third of the cases has it been found to be even a marginally significant factor, and this includes many situations where IRB financing in one state or town merely offsets its availability in another. That is, a plant would ordinarily have gone to Alabama, but Mississippi offers an enticing IRB tax-exempt subsidy. Then Alabama counters with its own IRB, so the plant is built there after all. Since almost every state provides this "free lunch" federal subsidy, this is not surprising, and—from an overall economic standpoint—not helpful, especially to federal taxpayers.

Besides their dubious benefits, industrial revenue bond use has hidden costs to the state. Excessive issuing of IRBs can push up general state borrowing costs (Kimball, 1976). The demand for tax-exempt bonds as an investment is not unlimited at the prevailing interest rate. As a larger volume of bonds comes into the market, buyers bearing the highest personal tax rates (and thus willing to accept the lowest interest rate) are not sufficient. To induce buyers with lower tax rates to purchase tax-exempt bonds, the interest rate paid to them must be increased. Thus large issues of IRBs one year may mean a state pays more next year to bond-finance construction of a hospital or school.

More subtly, but no less important, the "empty calories" a state government gets from an IRB program reduces its intake of truly effective development programs. It leads to a belief that something is being done to encourage economic development when nothing is really happening. This makes it less likely that other, worthwhile state programs will be undertaken.

Reforming the Use of Industrial Revenue Bonds

In recent years, there has been an attempt to reform the IRB mechanism. Rather than using these programs to *subsidize* capital costs, reforms have been undertaken to encourage their use in making more capital *available* to smaller firms suffering from financial market imperfections. Many states and localities believe that their IRB financing of smaller businesses now provides these firms with funds they otherwise would not obtain. While the motive is sound of transforming IRB programs into something that meets the needs of small firms poorly served by conventional lenders, in fact all but a handful of states have failed to introduce the changes necessary to make this happen.

Simply limiting the size of projects which can qualify for IRBs, as the Revenues and Expenditures Act that passed Congress in 1968 did, is not sufficient. This act permitted tax-exempt status for an IRB issue up to $1 million without any restrictions. Moreover, only issues up to $5 million for any one company can receive tax-exempt status, and then only if the recipient firm spends no more than $5 million for plant and equipment within the county over a period of three years before and three years after sale of the issue. (In 1978, this ceiling was raised to $10 million.) Also, in 1968, the SEC began requiring that publicly issued IRBs over $300,000 be registered according to the rules and publicly issued security must follow. Previously, publicly issued IRBs required no registration of this type.

The combined effect of this legislation has changed the size of firms receiving revenue bond financing. An analysis of IRBs listed in *Moody's Bond Records* (which tends to include only the relatively large, rated IRB public issues) showed the average size of an issue falling from $18.4 million in the pre-1968 period to $3.5 million in the post-1968 period (IILED, 1979).

But while IRBs are more often being used for local, smaller companies and less for Fortune 500 type firms, funds are still not getting to those small firms who really need them. Rather, IRB financing is going to those small enterprises who do not have much trouble with conventional sources. This is not surprising. Since conventional (or "self sustaining") revenue bonds are backed up only by the income the recipient business generates, they can only be used to finance a firm already perceived by the capital market as creditworthy.

Evidence confirming this situation can be found by looking at the manner in which IRBs are currently being sold. Almost all IRBs sold for small to medium-sized companies are private placements with local banks. In Alabama, for example, 86 percent of the issues for such firms are sold in this manner (IILED, 1979). Typically, firms needing capital and wanting the subsidy associated with IRBs go to their local banks, who aid them in dealing with the state and local bureaucracy. The local bank then purchases the bond issue. Little is offered that would cause the bank to make a loan it would have otherwise refused. Instead of making a conventional loan, the banks participate in order to serve their customers, who want the IRB subsidy. They lose nothing since the bonds have a competitive, after-tax return. In fact, the local bank often gains in two ways: *first,* they can carry the "loan" in their bond portfolio. This means they will be able to make more loans than otherwise would have been the case before exceeding their legally constrained loan-to-deposit ratio. And *second,* they gain that portion of the tax exemption they do not pass on to their customer. That is, the bank gives the customer a somewhat lower tax-exempt rate than loan rate, but not as low as they might. The difference is a slightly higher return to the bank. But typically the bank could get this by charging more interest on a straight loan to the company.

Revenue bonds for larger corporations—a third to half of all IRBs in some jurisdictions—continue to be handled by out-of-state investment bankers and underwriters, and frequently sold publicly.

So just placing a ceiling on the amount of individual IRB issues, or even the size of eligible companies, will not adequately transform industrial revenue bond intermediaries into capital-market-perfecting institutions. Something more must be done. The key change would appear to be offering some collateral or security to the bond purchaser beyond the future income of the recipient firm. There are two methods of providing this security. One is to insure the bonds with state mortgage insurance, and the other is to actually back the bonds with the full faith and credit of the state—that is, issuing general obligation bonds (or g.o. bonds, as they are commonly called) instead of revenue bonds.

Using General Obligation Bonds

In thirty-six states, issuing g.o. bonds to raise money for business loans simply cannot be done within the limits of the state constitution or statutes. These prohibitions arose in the wake of the 1870s economic crisis when railway and canal aid bonds sold by local governments ran into trouble. Revenue bonds—not requiring the full faith and credit of the state—represented a circumvention of these constitutional restrictions. For the large number of states having such prohibitions, state sponsored mortgage insurance for bonds must suffice.

Insuring Revenue Bonds

Currently at least six states—Arkansas, Connecticut, Maryland, Delaware, New Jersey and Massachusetts—offer insurance for revenue bond issues that would not otherwise be marketable. This insurance is provided through their state guarantee programs, and works in the same manner. It is important to note that the states which cannot use g.o. bonds for business financing are usually the same ones which are unable to pledge such bonding authority to back up their guarantees. So these states, unlike others, must start out with a sizable, legislatively appropriated insurance fund to assure industrial revenue bond buyers that defaults on insured bonds will be covered in full.

In Massachusetts, $2 million was appropriated to begin its Industrial Mortgage Insurance Program fund. This is the fund that backs revenue bond issues, as well as being the backbone for the regular guarantee program.

In New Jersey, the insured IRBs are secured by a loan guarantee fund of $10 million set up in 1975. In 1977, eight of eleven New Jersey Economic Development Authority guarantees were for revenue bonds. NJEDA, however, can only guarantee a maximum of 30 percent of an IRB or up to $1 million, whichever is less. The Massachusetts Industrial Finance Agency has more flexibility. MIFA is empowered to insure up to 90 percent of a bond or loan, but in practice usually only insures 40 percent. MIFA's aim is to insure only what is needed to encourage the bank to make the loan or bond.

Having only insurance fund support for insured IRBs, as opposed to deeper backup such as general obligation bonds, means that the fund must be large in relation to the total volume of borrowing it secures. NJEDA, for instance, is unable to secure more than three times the fund's assets. When talking about revenue bonds, that's not very much, although some other state programs, such as the one in Massachusetts, can insure up to ten times the revenue fund.

When g.o. bonds can be used for business financing, either no insurance at all is required, since the bonds already have the full credit of the state behind them, or the insurance fund can be *much* smaller, since bond purchasers know that the state treasury is available should the fund be unable to cover all defaults. Fourteen states currently authorize g.o. bond financing of business lending.

A Key Innovation: "Umbrella" Revenue Bond Financing

The best developed program for small enterprise backed by some level of general obligation bonding is the Umbrella Revenue Bond Program, operated since 1973 as a part of the Connecticut Development Authority (CDA). The program's title is something of a misnomer, since, at least in the last analysis, a *general obligation* bond can be issued by CDA to back up a group of industrial development mortgage loans, if intermediate forms of security fail to protect the investor. Financing under this program is supposed to go to small, high-risk firms unable to qualify for regular, "self sustaining" industrial revenue bonds backed only by their own credit.

State policy makers need to have a clear understanding of the nature of the security behind CDA's umbrella revenue bond program. On the one hand, the principles it embodies deserve emulation by many states. On the other hand, CDA's own experience would suggest that the extent and depth of security is far in excess of what is actually necessary to protect a reasonably prudent, well-informed bond purchaser. As a practical matter, however, the mere presence of heavily backed CDA umbrella revenue bonds in the public market place will discourage risk averse bond purchasers from buying more carefully tailored, but less heavily secured, umbrella bonds issued by other states. Moreover, as we shall see, the degree of risk aversion in tax-exempt revenue bond markets is often shocking.

To begin with, CDA umbrella bonds exhibit the best market-perfecting qualities of risk spreading and pooling, and include efficiencies which reduce information and transaction costs. CDA umbrella bonds usually pool twenty or more small loans in one large bond issue. To the extent that these small firms represent a wide range of different industries which have differing sensitivities to the business cycle, this pool of risks is reasonably diversified with regard to unsystemic risk (although these are, still, all small Connecticut corporations).

Next, the umbrella revenue bond issue which pools all of these diverse risks is sold in the public bond market. Selling the issue publicly has two salient aspects: first, selling the issue publicly further spreads the risks among many bond purchasers, each of whom purchases a small portion of the whole portfolio, and an even smaller portion of each individual loan in the pool. Such spreading is intermediate to more effective pooling in each individual bondholder's portfolio. Thus, umbrella revenue bonds exhibit both essential mechanisms for portfolio risk reduction—spreading and pooling.

Second, selling the bond publicly (rather than placing the bonds privately as so many state programs such as Pennsylvania and Maryland do) simultaneously avoids substituting one loan in the state for another, and may import "foreign" capital into the state.

Also, CDA, with a relatively large and experienced staff, reduces the information costs to near zero for the bond buyer. CDA staff carefully screen and evaluate all credits, so that, in effect, the bond buyer invests in CDA and CDA's judgment, not in the individual credit. From a market-perfecting standpoint, this central credit evaluation is quite efficient, and all of CDA's staff and administrative costs are covered by the fees paid by the firms receiving the loans covered by the bonds.

Finally, by *combining* lots of small loans into one large bond, CDA substantially reduces the legal, accounting and SEC filing fees borne by any single small borrower. For any one of the borrowers, those public market transaction costs would be prohibitive. Spread among the pool, the substantially lowered costs per borrower become affordable.

These market-perfecting efficiencies help to reduce risk and thus increase the security of a bond buyer's investment. But for CDA, they are just the beginning. In addition, CDA provides four "water-levels" of additional protection to every bond holder. The critical public policy question is, are all of these levels of security really necessary?

The first level of security is in the bond issue itself. For every $1,000,000 borrowed, the borrower only has the use of $850,000, leaving the balance in a reserve against loss. This is common financial practice. When one borrows $1,000,000 from the bank, one has to put up 20 percent (or $200,000) in compensating balances; the cost is the same since the borrower only gets to use $800,000. Thus, twenty $850,000 loans (or $17,000,000) provide a reserve within the $20,000,000 umbrella bond itself of $3,000,000. That alone is enough to permit 2½ complete failures, without reaching for any further security. Those are high odds, indeed!

The next level of security is CDA's own mortgage insurance. Like New Jersey and Massachusetts, Connecticut is authorized to issue mortgage insurance for revenue bonds, and does so for its own "umbrella" revenue bonds. On top of that, CDA's revenue bonds are backed by the accumulated reserves of CDA itself. And, on top of that, CDA has the standby *authority* to issue general obligation bonds of the state to "fill up" any default that might sink through all of those levels of security.

Not surprisingly, CDA has never needed to use this "fill up" provision for any umbrella revenue bond. This is clearly a case of overkill which says far more about the risk averseness of the industrial revenue bond market, and the lack of sophisticated information available to it, than it does about the soundness of financing small, growing, profitable enterprises.

As one measure of the risk aversion of the public marketplace, the Massachusetts Industrial Finance Agency (MIFA) has the authority to issue umbrella revenue bonds backed by all of the levels of security CDA has, except the "fill up" provision of the state's full faith and credit general obligation bonds. (Massachusetts is one of those thirty-six states whose constitution prohibits it from backing private credit with the state's full faith and credit.) MIFA has never been able to issue an umbrella revenue bond. Alaska is now exploring the possibility of issuing umbrella revenue bonds backed by a substantial stream of oil revenues, rather than "full faith and credit." It will be interesting to see the market's reaction.

Connecticut's umbrella program, as we have noted, only lends up to $850,000 for land and building financing and $500,000 for related machinery financing. Between 1973 and June 1977, it supplied loans to 67 businesses totaling $24.4 million. The financings ranged from $33,000 to $900,000, with a $300,000 average—more than ten times smaller than the current national average for regular IRBs (using Moody's figures, which are biased upward).

Putting Connecticut's Experience in Perspective

Much comment has been made about the absence of defaults by participating firms during the CDA umbrella program's first five years. One school of thought argues this reflects how perverse the barriers are preventing such firms from getting conventional financing, and how effectively CDA has overcome them in the umbrella program. In fact, CDA spends a great deal of staff resources and expense on the screening process by which loan applicants are reviewed. This willingness to accept high information and transactions costs, while charging the borrower accordingly, represents a major distinction between this public intermediary and private lenders. Moreover, CDA may be becoming so specialized and experienced in this small business lending process that it is doing the job more efficiently as well.

But the absence of defaults may also reflect an undesirable degree of risk aversion on the part of the authority, causing it to screen out a class of small borrowers, who, while riskier, offer a return that justifies financing them. CDA is sometimes described as a more conservative lender than commercial banks in the state.

While we have emphasized the need to offer greater bond security, it has been argued that simply packaging the revenue bond issues of riskier, small firms would be sufficient to improve their marketability. While it is true that such packaging, as practiced by CDA, can reduce the overall transaction costs of issuing IRBs, packaging *alone* will probably not lead to the funding of businesses which were not financable before. Simply put, without bond insurance, g.o. bond backing, or both, the bond purchasers still feel the need to look at every company in the package, producing very large information costs. More important, whatever risk pooling opportunity the packaging yields to an investor, it is highly doubtful that these would change a prior perception that such firms are too risky to invest in, if that was the barrier to their conventional financing in the first place. Clearly, the current level of risk aversion of the tax-exempt bond market calls for unduly high levels of security, as CDA's experience demonstrates.

DEBT INTERMEDIARIES FINANCED THROUGH TAX REVENUE

Our discussion of bond-financed debt intermediaries has shown that creating sound state-owned financial institutions is no simple matter. Tax-financed public lending institutions further illustrate the tradeoffs that must be made in designing effective business financing programs. On the one hand, because they are funded independently of the private capital market, they have greater freedom to abandon the undesirable behavior of conventional lenders; this allows them to better serve capital-starved small firms. On the other hand, this freedom can permit new kinds of inefficiency, as well as entailing other costs.

Direct Loan Programs These intermediaries are commonly re-
Financed Only ferred to as *direct loan programs* since
by Taxes they do not require raising capital by way
of the bond market. Direct loan programs have been introduced increasingly during the 1960s and early 1970s: fifteen now exist for financing plant construction and eleven for financing equipment. Where state constitutions forbid loans to for-profit business, these programs loan through local non-profit development authorities.

In many cases, direct loan programs serve as a vehicle for interest subsidies, as IRBs do. Most lend at rates near or under the below-market, tax-exempt bond rate. For example, the Pennsylvania Industrial Development Authority (PIDA) typically charges a 4 percent interest rate, and can go down as far as 1/2 percent. Since direct loan programs do not have to pay regular or tax-exempt market rates to raise their funds, they can afford to charge borrowers these lower rates.

To the extent these subsidies do not influence interstate investment location, and the evidence suggests they rarely do, this interest rate flexibility simply leads to a greater squandering of funds than would occur through bond-financed programs. More important, this subsidy comes out of the *state's* tax revenues, not the federal government's, as in the case of IRBs.

A few states attempt to target these loans geographically, so the subsidies may have some positive impact on intrastate location, an issue we take up in Chapter 8.

Despite their use as locational subsidy vehicles, the potential advantage of direct loan programs over IRBs could be in serving capital-deprived, profitable small firms otherwise cut off from capital access. *First,* because they are not accountable to private capital markets for their funds, tax-financed loan authorities are potentially free to invest in firms conventional lenders do not like, despite their underlying soundness. State direct loan programs can, like that in Vermont, actually require outright that a business must have had its loan request already rejected twice by conventional sources in order to qualify for aid. But the contrary danger is that such a bureaucratically managed program either becomes too insensitive to the marketplace and lends money to unsound firms who should not receive more capital at all. *Second,* if the funds lent by direct loan programs are not taken from capital that would have been lent or invested in other firms (but instead come out of personal taxation) there is far less chance that the recipient business will simply be displacing another firm.

It would appear on the surface that tax-financed state intermediaries are capable of being more successful in reaching firms for whom capital availability is a problem. While direct evidence on this point is skimpy, these programs are making riskier loans than either bond-financed or commercial lenders, as reflected in their typically higher loss rates. However, around this higher average there has been a lot of variation in the loss rates of direct loan programs—some high and others extremely low.

Part of this diversity may reflect the erratic or conservative behavior that may be injected into the management of these institutions as a result of their dependency on annual appropriations and thus on their political vulnerability. This may force some state loan managers to become more conservative than the private market for fear of political criticism. Conversely, it may force other fund managers to be more sensitive to political judgments as to who gets what loans where than sound economic development would suggest.

The largest tax-financed state lender, the Pennsylvania Industrial Development Authority, has experienced extraordinarily low losses. PIDA has written off only $52,000 out of $428.7 million in loans between 1956 and 1976. Many people in Pennsylvania interviewed in the course of a recent study, however, declared that PIDA was more stringent than commercial banks in the state.

Less soluble may be the political problem of taking sizable chunks of tax revenue for these programs. The fact is, except for PIDA, the volumes of loans made annually by direct loan programs is much smaller than that of bond-financed intermediaries.

For example, many of the programs, like that in Texas, receive a one-time "grant of principal" of only a few million dollars. They then operate as revolving funds. As loans are paid back, the money goes into the loan authority's kitty to be re-lent. Such direct loan programs do not have to receive supplemental appropriations to survive and grow moderately, but they must receive annual appropriations if they are to grow rapidly. A direct loan program charging 6 percent interest would take approximately twelve years to double its assets. So even though PIDA has paralyed $188 million in appropriations between 1956 and 1972 into a $325 million fund, it found itself having to go to the bond market in 1975 when further tax appropriations seemed out of the question.

Direct Loan Programs Financed by Taxes Combined With Other Sources

The vicissitudes of tax financing argue for direct loan programs seeking additional compatible sources of funds. One possible source is state pension funds: the Kentucky direct loan program borrowed $2.1 million from their public employee retirement fund. Alaska's direct loan program has borrowed millions from its natural resource endowment funds, so much, in fact, that the state direct loan programs are referred to as Alaska's second largest bank.

Another source is the federal government: Minnesota's revolving loan fund obtained 75 percent of its capital from the Economic Development Administration.

Finally, there is the bond market. Having an existing direct loan program go to the bond market for part of its capital is not necessarily equivalent to setting up a bond-financed intermediary from scratch. If the program has earned a sound reputation, then it can issue special obligation bonds, as PIDA has done to the tune of $72.5 million. These bonds fall somewhere between revenue bonds and general obligation bonds, avoiding some of the pitfalls of each. They are secured by all the income and assets of the issuing agency, not just the revenues of the specific firms they finance, but do not require the full faith and credit of the state.

In many cases, a shortfall of appropriations for tax-financed intermediaries has not been a barrier to their growth. Just the opposite, funds have exceeded demand. This situation results from a combination of these programs' newness, their lack of effective publicity, their occasional reputation for conservatism, and perhaps most important, their extreme centralization.

Again, PIDA can be seen as the exception that proves the rule. It has excess demand, but also happens to be effectively decentralized through eighty local industrial development authorities (IDAs) at the county and municipal level. These IDAs assume much of the responsibility in originating loans to firms in their communities.

In summary, the experience of direct loan programs is extremely mixed. Their lack of need to adhere to strict market sensitivity gives them the potential to undertake substantial risk. Most direct loan programs have responded to that opportunity either by being far more conservative than they need be, or far less financially sound than they ought to have been.

Once again, rarely do interest subsidies make any sense, especially to the state taxpayers funding them. Some programs, of which PIDA is most noteworthy, increase the availability of capital to firms directly proportional to the extent of unemployment in the area of the state where they operate. This can induce credit starved, job generating small firms to start-up or expand in those very areas where they are most needed. We will analyze this approach further in Chapter 8.

EQUITY-PROVIDING INTERMEDIARIES

Regardless of how they are financed, state intermediaries that provide only debt—loans with fixed, regular repayment terms—cannot satisfy all the unmet small business capital needs. Any state that is serious about nurturing enterprises that have been unjustifiably refused funds from conventional sources must provide for equity financing as well. In contrast to the inexorable principal and interest repayments required of debt, equity represents capital supplied to a firm in return for some share of its uncertain future income. This type of financing gives brand new businesses or ones branching into new fields a critically necessary holiday from capital costs until they begin generating positive cash flows. It employs a whole variety of financial instruments, some of which eventually approach conventional debt.

From the perspective of the institution providing capital, equity financing is more difficult and challenging than debt financing, as we will see momentarily. So only a handful of pioneering states have recently established this type of public financial institution. This is in sharp contrast to nearly every European or Third World nation, or Canadian province, all of which have long standing experience with state capitalized, equity financing development banks. Despite their newness, these American experiments can already teach some important lessons.

Uses of Funds

Perhaps reflecting the negative lessons of past state financial intermediation, none of the equity providers chiefly functions to attract investment through capital subsidies. On the contrary, they are firmly grounded in the assumption that employment and income gains can be most cost-effectively achieved through redirecting funds toward capital-poor but competitive business enterprises. While sharing this common approach, they differ in their specific target firms.

The oldest of the equity providers, the Connecticut Product Development Corporation (CPDC), founded in 1973, does not try to invest in ventures that will directly employ a lot of people. Rather, its object is to "select development opportunities that will result in new products offering employment opportunities for Connecticut citizens." Viewing its comparative advantage as lying in technological innovation, the state hopes to trigger sectorial growth in its economy through assisting capital-poor firms that may open up new industries, CPDC invests in specific projects of a corporation, not in the firm as a whole. These are generally endeavors of relatively well-established firms, with 5 to 50 employees and $.5 to $2.5 million in sales, which are branching out into a new market. CPDC concentrates on funding expenditures at the development stage (between research and actual production), but has been moving more into the marketing and production stage as this later financing has not been as easily obtainable from private sources as anticipated.

Like its Connecticut cousin, the newly born Massachusetts Technology Development Corporation can only invest in businesses using a "significant amount of technology." However, MTDC is geared toward providing equity to young companies who have already engaged in product development to the point of needing production and distribution financing. It seeks more direct job-creation benefits than does CPDC, though it shares the notion of the state's comparative advantage lying in high technology.

Similarly designed to exploit its economy's long-run strong suit, the infant Alaska Renewable Resources Corporation (ARRC) will invest in firms that are developing products, markets or technologies which can become key elements of renewable resource-based enterprises. Such firms are defined by a resource base that can remain relatively constant over time, including agriculture, timber, fisheries and alternative "renewable energy sources such as water, solar and geothermal power. In addition, a company must be "economically viable" yet not be able to get sufficient capital from other sources on reasonable terms to qualify for ARRC financing. ARRC can help pay for research and development, and product demonstration, but not for actual production costs.

Both the Kentucky Highlands Investment Corporation (KHIC) and the Massachusetts Community Development Finance Corporation (CDFC) focus their equity investment in a different manner. They invest in new or expanding ventures that are located in economically depressed target areas. KHIC, founded in 1971, operates solely in a nine-county area of southeastern Kentucky containing 180,000 mostly poor and unskilled people. CDFC, operating since 1978, can provide financing only to community development corporation-sponsored ventures. These two institutions will be discussed much more extensively in Chapter 8, though we will have some further comments about them in this section.

Forms of Financing What separates this alphabet soup of institutions—the CPDC, PDC, MTDC, ARRC, KHIC, CDFC—from the scores of other intermediaries already discussed are the terms on which they supply capital to their target firms. Except for CPDC, all can employ any of four commonly used equity or equity-like financial instruments. One is pure *common stock*. In return for the funds common stock purchases provide, the institution receives a prorated share of any earnings of the recipient firm left after payment of taxes and interest. Another is *preferred stock*. In return for the funds common stock purchases provide, the institution receives a prorated share of any earnings. of the recipient before any one else. On the other hand, preferred stock carries no (or minimal) voting rights. The third instrument is *convertible debt*. Convertible debt differs from regular debt in that along with a commitment to interest and principal repayments, the borrower gives the lender the right to convert his debt notes into a certain amount of common stock on or before a certain date. Finally, there is *subordinated debt*. In the event of default, the subordinated lender is paid only after all the senior creditors, such as banks and insurance companies, who have prior claim on the firm's assets, are paid off.

Let us look at how each of these arrangements can benefit new and growing small firms. Common stock eliminates the burden of regular interest and principal repayments on an enterprise that may easily not have reached the point of a positive net income, as does preferred stock. The common stockholder, as an owner, is sharing with the entrepreneur the uncertain risks and rewards of future income or losses in the firm. Issuing preferred stock further guarantees that current owners' control of the firm will not be diluted. Both common and preferred stock carry relatively high risk since the investor can end up with little or nothing if the firm does poorly, but it offers the commensurate possibility of relatively high returns.

With convertible debt the investor has protection if the firm does poorly—interest and principal repayment plus a claim on the firm's assets if necessary—but the added bonus of an ownership share if the firm does well. This combination of "downside protection" and "upside potential" can make lending to a small firm attractive when it would otherwise be too risky. However, convertible debt may be less attractive than straight equity from the borrower's point of view since it imposes regular debt service requirements.

Subordinated debt (sometimes called subordinated debentures) has this undesirable feature as well; its unique benefit to the firm is that its subordinate position lessens the risk to others who might lend to the firm, possibly leveraging additional, private "senior"debt. In this way, it functions much like common or preferred stock can in a business's capital structure. To put it another way, from the senior bank lenders' viewpoint, the subordinated debt may be attractive because it looks like equity. Whereas, from the investor's viewpoint, the subordinated debt may be attractive because it looks like debt in comparison to riskier equity. From the owner-entrepreneur's viewpoint, the investor's subordinated debt is attractive because it looks like equity to the senior bank lender, but does not compromise the entrepreneur's ownership in the firm.

To summarize, these financing arrangements can provide more flexible repayment, special protection or opportunities that make an otherwise unattractive investment interesting, or help leverage other outside investment.

The one financial instrument left out—the *royalty agreement*—is used by CPDC in its financings and is also available to the ARRC, CDFC and TDC. CPDC pays 60 percent of a firm's product development costs; in return it receives a 5 percent royalty on the net sales of the firm for this product. This ceases when CPDC has gotten five times its initial contribution. Such a royalty has a number of advantages: it creates no claim on the firm until there is a positive cash flow from sales, and it does not compromise the ownership structure of the firm.

An excellent example of how these financial instruments can be used in combination can be seen in KHIC's financing of Outdoor Venture Corporation, a manufacturer of tents and recreational equipment. In 1972, KHIC purchased a 25 percent common stock stake for $100,000, and a six-year 14 percent subordinated debenture for $120,000 to help the firm get started. Four years later in 1976, it purchased a $250,000, two-year, 11 percent subordinated debenture (leveraging an additional senior bank line) and a $130,000 20-year mortgage participation to help OVC with expansion financing.

None of these institutions are designed to be the sole financers of the enterprise in which they invest. For example, CPDC is limited to funding 60 percent product development costs, and MTDC, ARRC and CDFC cannot own more than 49 percent of the voting stock in a firm. This ensures that outside, private funds are leveraged, and that the state institution does not actually end up managing the enterprise, a situation considered by the designers of such programs to be both politically untenable and inefficient. Other limitations ensure that the portfolios of these equity providers will have some degree of diversification, and that relatively small firms will be the ones assisted. These constraints are embodied in ceilings like ARRC's—no more than 5 percent of its capital or $1.5 million, whichever is less, may be put in a single project—or MTDC's—its initial investment cannot exceed $500,000 and lifetime investment more than $1,000,000 in a single business.

Sources of Funds

Regardless of what an equity-providing intermediary is envisioned as investing in, what it ends up doing will depend critically on how it is funded. We have previously noted that in finance, "you are what you eat." Short term sources of capital cannot be lent long without endangering either the borrowing firm or the development bank. Debt as a source cannot finance equity as a use, without similar troubles down the road. And tax financed grants are always a problem if one wants market sensitivity. This holds for these institutions just as it did for the debt intermediaries.

Two of the intermediaries, CPDC and CDFC, are financed through general obligation bond issues. Normally this would *not* be an appropriate source of funds since debt service payments on the bonds will be a constant demand while equity income or royalty income ebbs and flows. The catch is that the debt service payments come out of general state tax revenue, not the investment income of the institutions themselves. While that particular problem has been solved, an additional is created—not requiring the equity provider to pay for its funds means that it has less incentive to operate efficiently.

The same point can be made in regard to KHIC (financed by federal tax revenue), MTDC (financed by federal tax revenue via an EDA grant), and ARRC (financed by mineral lease bonuses and royalties, along with rental from state lands).

However, what may still act as an incentive to invest efficiently is the explicit or implicit reality that these institutions are not likely to receive subsequent bond financing or tax appropriations. If they do not invest in ventures that will at least return enough to maintain the equity fund, they will cease to exist. If they do not earn a positive return, they cannot grow. For example, CPDC is "to become self-sustaining through reimbursements from successful development."

One more issue is worth noting: while CPDC and CDFC both are financed out of g.o. bonds, the way they receive their financing is very different. CPDC gets its bonds authorized on an "as needed" basis; CDFC got $10 million all at once. The result is that CPDC is as dependent on bond financing as direct loan programs are on annual legislative authorizations. Thus CPDC cannot plan, cannot adequately finance its operations out of portfolio income, and is likely to be too dependent on the other concerns of the state treasury. CDFC, conversely, may be too independent of all these constraints.

Whatever the limitations of these sources of funds, they do represent the kind of "patient" money that would have been difficult to raise in private capital markets, at least until these institutions have a track record. The only other source of money that could wait for long-run, competitive returns would perhaps be public employee pension funds, whose possible contribution we will discuss in the next section.

Of special noteworthiness in evaluating the importance of where the money comes from is the case of MTDC. The original intention was to have MTDC financed by the same method used for CDFC. However, because MTDC financed private firms directly, rather than through community development corporations, MTDC violated Massachusetts' prohibition against using state credit to support private firms, as CDFC did not. Thus, on the basis of the state supreme court opinion on CDFC's g.o. bond financing, the final legislation for MTDC did not provide for this state backed general obligation funding. MTDC found itself left high and dry with a $150,000 state appropriation for operating expenses only.

Instead of the original plan—$10 million in general obligation bond financing—MTDC is now relying on a 5-year, $2 million grant from EDA (under its Title IV Special Economic Development and Assistance Revolving Loan Fund Program). But this money can only be used under severe constraints. It cannot be given out in equity form and can only be used for building and land financing. Since the funds will be supplied as debt, requiring fixed, periodic repayments, MTDC is biased away from start-ups and towards already existing firms wishing to expand their product lines. It is just this type of company that can draw on its existing, income-generating operations to service the debt in the early years; it is not the high risk, high return uncertain start-up MTDC was intended to finance.

Nevertheless, MTDC will be offering some very beneficial terms. The debt will be uncollateralized and subordinated, with the possibility of payment holidays (1 year for start-ups and 6 months for expansions). Loans will run for a maximum of 7 years, and cannot exceed $250,000.

Getting In and Getting Out

So far we have discussed issues that have their counterparts in the design of debt-providing intermediaries. For equity providers, there are the added issues of "getting in" and "getting out." "Getting in" refers to identifying and developing investment opportunities. Unlike debt intermediaries, equity intermediaries financing start-ups or very young firms do not always confront business plans set in concrete. There may not be much more than an entrepreneur and a good idea. Moreover, because in equity financing the ongoing performance of investments will determine the level of financial return, the institution has an even greater interest in seeking out good ventures and providing them with ongoing management consulting. These technical assistance functions should be the responsibility of a separate wing of the equity-providing institution or a wholly different organization. This will ensure that financing decisions are made independently of biases, pro and con, that may arise in the proposal development stage.

KHIC, for example, employs Venture Founders, Inc. (formerly the Institute for New Enterprise Development) of Belmont, Massachusetts and Columbus, Ohio on a more-or-less continuous retainer. Venture Founders locates and screens entrepreneurs, and gives the best ones technical assistance in developing business plans. The Outdoor Venture Corporation, discussed above, entered KHIC's portfolio through Venture Founders entrepreneurial recruitment and assessment program. CDFC suffered in its first year of operation because it did not have such an ally. Both ARRC and MTDC can spend money supporting opportunity identification technical assistance, if they choose to, and the KHIC has already chosen to enter into a similar management contract with Venture Founders. Only CPDC has no provisions for this, which is consistent with their focus on existing firms.

"Getting out" refers to how equity-providing intermediaries cash in on their investments. As we emphasize in Chapter 3, this has been a major problem in the venture capital market. One solution is simply to use financial instruments towards the debt end of the continuum. This, as well as royalty agreements, provide automatic repayment and earnings over time. For example, about 60 percent of Kentucky Highlands investments are in a debt-like form. The other approach involves what is known as a "put." When equity is advanced, an agreement is made that the financed firm must buy back the stock at some fixed price at a certain future date. This price will reflect a reasonable return to the equity provider, who can exercise this *option* if it cannot sell its shares to another investor for a larger gain. In general, exit is not as great a problem for public as compared to private venture capitalists, since their "investors" (i.e., taxpayers) do not put on pressure for liquidity.

In evaluating the overall merits of existing models for equity-providing state intermediaries, the most that can be said is that they exhibit some well-designed features but will have to mature before their success can be determined.

For example, since 1974, CPDC has committed $1.4 million and approved 19 projects. Based on its initial cash flow projections: 35 percent of supported projects will succeed, project size will average $100,000, and the typical successful project will produce no revenues for two years, grow for three years, with positive revenues, and support royalty payments at constant mature volume for six more years. Like the experience of British National Research and Development Corporation, it expects a number of years before its portfolio shows profits.

MTDC expects that with its $2 million EDA revolving loan fund, forty-eight firms will be assisted in the first five years. Ten of these will fail and the rest succeed. Twenty-nine will have been start-ups and nineteen expansions.

Encouragement can be found in the record of KHIC, the oldest of these institutions. It has eleven major business ventures in its portfolio, employing several hundred people, almost all of whom were on unemployment or welfare. These businesses had 1977 annual sales of $11.7 million, and four already have national markets. KHIC has provided them $3.09 million in debt and equity, and there has been an additional $3.00 invested for every KHIC dollar. By 1977 it had a net unrealized gain of $475,000 on its portfolio, and the only loss has been a $47,000 loan made in 1973 to a feeder pig cooperative.

STATE AND LOCAL PUBLIC FUNDS AS A SOURCE OF DEVELOPMENT CAPITAL

So far, we have been talking about the state government's role in more effectively channeling other people's savings into job-generating business enterprises, whether it be through the use of administrative regulation, economic incentives or direct state intermediation. But the state has its "own" savings to think about as well. How can state and local public funds be a source of development capital?

This issue is important because of the large amount of capital entrusted to state and local funds, and because of the direct authority of state officials in determining how those funds are to be invested. The funds which the state controls are of two kinds: those balances held relatively temporarily for expenditures within the normal annual operations of the government, and those balances held in trust for disbursement further into the future. The short-term money comes from revenues exceeding expenditures during certain periods, such as just after tax collections or bond sales. The longer-term money represents the contribution of public employers and employees to state and local worker pension funds, or the large coal, natural gas and oil royalties and severance taxes now accruing in vast amounts to such diverse Western states as Texas, Montana and Alaska.

Short-Term versus Long-Term Funds

How much money is involved? Operating account balances cannot be estimated precisely, but at any one time during the fiscal year, they amount to about one-third of the annual state revenue. In 1975 these operating accounts amounted to about $50 billion. Public employee retirement system (PERS) assets now total over $100 billion. This year alone Alaska's oil income from taxes and royalties will double from $1 billion to $2 billion, and next year they will double again. Although less dramatic in other Western states, energy and mineral lease income represents a large new source of capital for investment.

In terms of the capital markets as a whole, these various public funds are quantitatively significant. For example, in June 1975 the total deposits of state and local funds in commercial banks represented 8.8 percent of those financial institutions' deposits. But it is only in the last two years that serious question has been raised about the economic use.

Operating account funds at the state level are generally managed by the treasurer, normally an elected official. An appointed investment committee usually oversees the general handling of pension funds, with day-to-day management often contracted out to private money managers. In some states, funds must simply be invested according to the prudent person rule, while in others there are more specific constitutional or statutory requirements, either laying out procedures or precise allocations of funds among different assets. Pension funds are also usually subject to rules requiring them to be invested in the interest of the retirement system participants. Only in exceptional cases do state economic development concerns directly enter into how this money is invested.

Where are these monies currently invested? Different patterns of investment prevail for short-term operating funds, as compared to long-term pension funds and royalty or severance tax income. The main assets of operating funds tend to be certificates of deposit in banks, treasury bills and commercial paper. Of state-administered pension funds, over one-half are in corporate bonds, approximately one-quarter in corporate stocks, and the remainder in mortgages and government securities. Both types of funds are managed to maximize yield given the desired amount of liquidity and risk exposure.

In the case of operating funds, liquidity in investment is much more important. Cash flows in and out of the state treasury cannot be precisely predicted. If operating balances are placed in illiquid assets, difficult to cash in on short notice, the state might have to borrow on unfavorable terms. So this money is generally put in the bank, as a regular time deposit, certificate of deposit, or demand deposit, or into commercial paper, certificates of deposit, or treasury bills.

Both types of funds are managed with a relatively intense degree of risk aversion and resultant low return. Public officials do not want to be saddled with the political liability of an investment loss, even if it is in a long-term asset that will eventually produce a high net gain, nor do they want to jeopardize what are the bulk of workers' retirement nest eggs in the case of pension funds.

Stimulating in-state economic development has not been an objective of these monies. A key question is, will more development-oriented investment require a lower financial return? Reduced liquidity? Higher risk? Higher transaction costs? How does the state determine the degree to which state economic development concerns and these other objectives are traded off? How can these trade-offs be minimized?

Direct versus Indirect returns

Whether state operating account and trust funds must give up financial return depends, first of all, on the type of use that is to be made of them. We have gone to great lengths in previous chapters to show that business enterprises do exist which are both in need of funds because of their poor treatment by conventional sources and yet do offer competitive risk-adjusted rates of return. If these are the type of investment that some public money gets shifted to, then, at worst, what is involved is moving to both a higher level of risk *and* a commensurately higher financial return. How far a fund should move in this direction depends on how one evaluates the risk aversion of the state taxpayers on whom gains and losses ultimately fall.

In contrast to this situation of investing in competitive but neglected opportunities within the state, there are certain socially oriented investments that would involve a lower financial return to operating account funds or pension funds. These include some depressed area investments of the type that will be outlined in Chapter 8. But even here the lower *direct* return may be offset by a higher *indirect* return. Put simply, the economic activity induced by the socially oriented investment may give the state increased tax revenue and reduce social welfare expenditure that outweigh the loss in interest, dividends or capital gains generated. Thus the "total return" may be competitive.

For these investments, especially in the case of pension funds where the trustees of the fund have a legal fiduciary responsibility to the employees who are beneficial owners of the fund the state government may have to commit itself to make available to the operating balance on pension funds a portion of the indirect return sufficient to raise their earnings to the appropriate level. In other words, the state must subsidize the investment with tax revenues. Such a case is under discussion in Alaska today. If the U.S. Congress should eliminate federal tax exemption for bonds financing single-family homes, it will profoundly affect the local housing market. One solution is for the Alaska Permanent Fund (financed by surplus oil revenues) to pick up a portion of the slack, along with state employee retirement funds. If so, the difference in rate of return would be borne by general appropriations of tax revenues.

Besides risk-adjusted rate of return trade-offs, there is also the question of sacrificing liquidity. This may be a serious restriction on the use of operating account funds to invest in long-term development-nurturing assets. Loans or stock or bond purchases from smaller firms and projects would not be easily cashable in the short term. This is not a serious restriction for pension funds, and is perhaps their main superior characteristic as a source of development capital. Their payouts are scattered over the long term. They can afford to invest in assets whose return is similarly spread out or delayed.

Investing Funds in Long-Term Development

As we have argued, development-oriented investment is a very specialized activity, and to have operating account or trust fund administrators doing it on their own would entail excessive transaction and information costs. If a state decides to increase the flow of public funds into either (1) neglected, but financially competitive, in-state investments or (2) socially desirable, but total return competitive projects, it has to choose appropriate vehicles or intermediaries for doing it. At the beginning, we can rule out those conventional state-chartered, general purpose financial intermediaries and markets whose imperfections constitute the very rationale for the state's decision to intervene. Remaining as the chief alternatives are the special purpose private intermediaries and public financial intermediaries described in previous sections of this study. Some conventional private institutions that distinguish or commit themselves to desired high-risk lending and investment may also be worth special state support. This latter approach is the intention of so-called "linked-deposit" programs. We shall discuss each of these possibilities below.

Investments in Federally Guaranteed Loans. The most popular development-oriented use of public employee retirement system funds so far has been to create a secondary market for federally guaranteed loans such as those of the Economic Development Administration (EDA), Farmers Home Administration (FmHA), Federal Housing Authority (FHA), Veterans Administration (VA), and Small Business Administration (SBA). For example, as of June 1978, the Kansas pension system had $9 million of its $600 million fund in SBA guarantee portions of loans made by Kansas banks. These are purchased through the brokerage of the Kansas Development Credit Corporation. This was permitted under the "prudent man" concept operative in Kansas. KDCC argues that their function as an "investment banker" of these federally guaranteed loans has substantially increased bank lending to small enterprise. The object of these secondary market programs is to increase the liquidity of these loans from the private lender's perspective, so that its preference for them will increase and its demand for the guaranteed loans will grow, and to boost the flow of funds to the lenders who have shown a propensity to make such loans.

Such secondary market operations, while fiduciarily sound, contribute little to state economic development if the guaranteed loans would have been purchased by others. In general, demand for any class of investments, once guaranteed, will be forthcoming. However, there are exceptions.

In a well-developed capital market such as Boston's, one would presume a well-functioning market was already fully made by private investment bankers. But a recent survey showed this not to be the case. Small "country" banks in Massachusetts held $300 million in such federal paper which they were prepared to sell. If they then reinvested some of their newly liquid funds in small firms, new development and job creation might result. As of 1977, the Hawaii PERS had 2.7 percent of its $836 million fund in purchases of low and moderate income housing mortgages guaranteed by the Hawaii Housing Authority. In this case, private investors had avoided purchasing the guaranteed instruments for reasons that are unclear. Here the pension fund investment may help to make capital available that otherwise would not have been.

Investments in Tax-Exempt State Bond Programs. What about investing public money in state public lending institutions? Investment in the obligations of bond-financed state debt intermediaries does not make sense for a tax-exempt investor like public pension funds as long as the bonds being sold are in turn tax-exempt ones. However, if these intermediaries begin issuing taxable obligations this could be an important contribution to solving capital market misallocation. Kentucky direct loan program's $2.1 million sale of debt notes to the state pension fund illustrates the practicality type of arrangement.

Investments in Direct Loan Programs. Both the Alaska housing case example cited above and the Kentucky direct loan program suggest the possibility of using large state pension or natural resource funds to finance direct loan programs now generally financed out of annual tax revenues.

Alaska has adopted a variation on this theme: A small appropriated reserve fund stands behind the sale of *all* Alaska's direct loans to the state treasury, who buys them with excess long-term oil revenues in one of the natural resource endowment funds. All servicing is provided by the loan program, and any loans in default are repurchased and, if necessary, liquidated through the small appropriated reserve.

Although this program has been exceedingly well managed, it does raise a number of basic issues: First, the large portfolio (it is equal to the second largest bank in Alaska) is not systematically diversified against risk; all loans are small and in Alaska. Large numbers are in highly vulnerable industries such as salmon fishing. The best loan fund management in the world cannot manage for a poor salmon run.

Second, despite the best efforts of the fund management, which has sought to establish an unsubsidized floating interest rate, the legislature has insisted on a 9.5 percent rate now a full four points below Alaska's prime.

Finally, the state is using scarce and valuable instate dollars to finance risks which a soundly constructed umbrella revenue bond program could use to import capital into this very capital-shy state economy.

Investments in Equity Financing Intermediaries. Perhaps the greatest potential of public money lies in pension fund financing of state equity capital funds. While there have been no examples of this, one state has invested in a number of private venture capital partnerships. As of June 1978, the State Teachers Retirement System of Ohio had .2 percent of its $4 billion assets in six national venture capital firms. These investments are partnerships which will terminate at the end of 1984, when the assets will be split. The Ohio Revised Code set criteria for eligible investments which were conceived to be broad enough to include the use of funds for such relatively high-risk, high-return equity investments. Although the returns to date have been commensurate with risk, the Ohio Attorney General has disallowed the future use of such state fiduciary funds.

Investing Public Funds in More Liquid Assets None of the state financial intermediaries described so far appear to be suitable for the sizable amount of operating balance funds currently invested in bank deposits and government securities. They require money to be tied up for a longer period than most state treasuries can afford to do. What is needed is a more liquid use of the money, that still makes some contribution to state economic development. Two responses are worth considering. One is a state-owned bank as a depository of these balances, the other is their "linked deposit" in commercial banks in the state.

Thinking About Establishing a State-Owned Bank. The single example of a state-owned, controlled and operated bank is the Bank of North Dakota. Founded in 1919 as a product of a long-standing populist movement demand, the Bank of North Dakota is now the largest bank in the state, with 10 percent of all deposits. It holds all the operating balance of the state and 10 percent of the localities' money. Together these sources account for 88 percent of the Bank of North Dakota's deposit base, the rest being time and demand deposits of individuals.

The Bank of North Dakota's performance in the area of business financing is questionable. The bank is prohibited from making direct business loans by its charter. It can make federally guaranteed VA and FHA home loans and student loans. These account for the largest share of its assets (21 percent). Also, it can participate in loans initiated by private lenders in the state and devotes 19 percent of its assets to this. Finally, it purchases the guaranteed portion of SBA loans made by other lenders in the state (3 percent). The balance of its resources, about one-half of the bank's assets, is in out-of-state investments—government and money market securities.

Neither the direct guaranteed home loans nor the secondary market for guaranteed loans represent very unique contributions to the provision of capital in a state, as noted above. More important are the loan participations: the state has many small rural banks whose legal lending limit or own-participation in loans to any one borrower is relatively small. Thus with the Bank of North Dakota's sharing in the transaction much larger loans can be made.

Even if the Bank of North Dakota were permitted to make direct business loans, it still would have trouble channeling more of its deposits into loans as opposed to out-of-state investments. The variability of its deposit base simply restricts the amount of money it can tie up in medium to long-term uses. Perhaps it could channel more deposits into short-term working capital loans if the prohibition on direct lending were removed. Moreover, it might rely on "bought money" or certificates of deposit to diversify its sources of funds. With these reforms, the bank would still be hamstrung by the fact it has only one office, in Bismarck, not the state's largest city, and no branches in other areas.

Evaluating Linked Deposit Systems. The other progressive alternative for the employment of bank-deposited operating balance funds is the linked-deposit system. Illinois introduced its linked-deposit system in 1967, Colorado in 1975 and Missouri in 1973. Missouri discontinued its program in 1976. These programs *link* the deposit of public funds to the lending behavior of depository institutions. Money is shifted toward those banks whose policies are deemed to be especially contributing to state economic development. These funds are intended, first, to increase the amount of funds these banks have to lend; and second, to provide them with an incentive to expand such loans. The incentive comes from the fact that an extra dollar of deposits in a bank represents an extra dollar on which it can earn the "spread" between its interest paid and interest received.

Any linked-deposit system has three components: determining which public funds are available for deposit, choosing which depository institutions are eligible to bid for them, and setting criteria and procedures for allocating funds among them. The last component is by far the most important, as it targets the funds. It is usually assumed that funds must be available for at least six months deposit if they are to be linked-deposit-system allocated.

While no linked-deposit system has been soundly evaluated, they have been subjected to a substantial amount of criticism as being ineffective. There is no guarantee that the bank will use the deposits for in-state lending beyond what the state could do on its own through public intermediaries of the type discussed above. The state has no way of determining this *ex post;* if the bank increases its loans in favored categories after receiving public deposits, it could easily be due to other factors. The converse holds as well. The key point is that the public deposits are *fungible*.

It is doubtful that the economic incentive embodied in the linked-deposit system is strong enough to overcome historical risk aversion, discriminatory practices, aversion to high transaction costs and other factors that would keep a conventional lender from making certain types of loans desirable from the state's perspective. Moreover, in most states, collateralization requirements on public deposits mean that banks must expand their reserve accounts to the point that a net outflow of funds from the state could be produced by a linked-deposit system. This is not to say that linked-deposit systems are not preferable to a random depositing of public money in state depository institutions; but they probably do not equal the overall return to a state of a sound daily cash management and sophisticated short-term investment portfolio such as those operated by Oregon, Wisconsin, and Minnesota.

7

OPTIONS FOR FINANCING HOUSING AND INFRASTRUCTURE

Business enterprises are not the only projects important to state economic development which suffer from capital market imperfections. Housing and public infrastructure can be essential ingredients in the development process, and often are plagued by similar kinds of capital market failures.

Although the importance of the housing *construction* industry to sound economic development is often overstressed, the importance of the *location* and *quality* of housing to expanded markets and labor supply is often understated. Housing construction jobs provide temporary, not permanent, employment, in contrast to industry and commerce. And the number of persons required to service, sell, manage and maintain housing once it is constructed is quite small.

But markets follow people, and people in part follow housing; and the people housed are the most important factor of production, labor. So housing can and does have a major impact on both markets (on the demand side) and the cost and availability of labor (on the supply side).

Moreover, government policies which affect the location and quality of housing can have a significant impact on local market demand and labor supply. Thus FHA's and VA's massive single family mortgage insurance programs contributed substantially to rapid postwar suburbanization and the disintegration of the inner city. Similarly, counter efforts by such able state development finance institutions as the Massachusetts Housing Finance Agency (MHFA) have contributed to the rebirth of old cities like Boston and Lowell through a conscious policy of financing the rehabilitation of high quality, mixed-income housing in their downtowns.

Infrastructure is equally important to profitable enterprise. Without roads, ports, heat, light, water and sewerage, key resources and investment opportunities remain untapped in underdeveloped rural areas and regions. Without reinvestment in disintegrating urban infrastructure, opportunities for central city renaissance go unrealized.

It is critical, however, that productive investment in business enterprise be tied to infrastructure investment, if such failed public policies as EDA's empty industrial parks in Appalachia, or HUD's still vacant urban renewal lots (left over from the fifties and sixties) are to be avoided. States investing in infrastructure to stimulate economic development can insist that no infrastructure finance will be undertaken which is not tied to a direct investment in job-creating enterprise.

In Chapter 3 we saw that both housing and infrastructure often suffer from the same kinds of capital market imperfections as small enterprise. These needs often go unmet because of inadequate mechanisms for pooling and spreading risks, too high information and transaction costs, local monopoly capital markets, and of course, prejudice. This is largely because single family home mortgages and many public works bonds amount to relatively small financings. The private market is often not as efficient as it might be in combining these individual small credits into larger, cheaper and more easily saleable lots.

These problems get worse when the loans are for properties in minority communities or projects in small outlying areas. In these kinds of places, there are likely to be only one or two banks who control the market; they usually would prefer not to make the loan at all, rather than take a higher return for a higher risk. And even if there are larger, more competitive banks available, they often find it too easy to take the lazy way out—simply code all blacks or small towns as poor risks, instead of investing more time and energy to make discriminate choices.

It is not surprising to find that state governments have responded to these problems by employing many of the same kinds of tools used to stimulate industrial and commercial development. States have tried to stimulate housing and public works by changing administrative regulation, implementing their own subsidy and guarantee programs, and creating new state housing finance agencies and municipal bond banks. In the following section key models and options for regulatory intervention are examined and economic incentives and new development banks are weighed, first for housing finance and then infrastructure.

FINANCING HOUSING

In the post war decades, every level of government has involved itself in financing housing construction and ownership. Much of this activity has centered around subsidizing the cost and increasing the availability of capital for multi-family rental units, especially for low and moderate income people. This will be discussed in the next chapter. More recently, there is an emerging recognition that capital market imperfections prevent many families from financing home ownership, even when they can pay the costs that an efficient market would demand of them. With this issue we will concern ourselves now.

Administrative Regulation   In the 1970s a state regulatory whirlwind began to sweep through housing finance markets. Some types of regulation have been tightened up; others have been relaxed. Throughout, the common theme has been to increase the availability of mortgage credit to individuals who should get it in a well-functioning capital market. Most visible have been so-called "anti-redlining" codes, designed to combat lending practices that *unjustifiably* restrict home mortgage credit for borrowers with certain personal characteristics or with property in certain neighborhoods. At the same time, lenders in many states have been given greater freedom in setting mortgage interest rates, since pre-existing rules sometimes prevented them from charging rates sufficient to compensate for the risks and costs involved in certain mortgage transactions. Two key "price de-control" changes here have been the introduction of floating usury ceilings and variable rate mortgages. We will look at both of these efforts to ease pricing regulation, after first looking at the movement to tighten up against redlining.

Anti-redlining codes: A well-functioning housing finance market would allocate mortgage credit on the basis of the fundamental credit-worthiness of the applicant, including the security offered by the property being purchased. Borrowers with higher default risk or greater transaction costs would have the terms of their mortgages—interest rate and duration—adjusted to reflect these facts. The essence of "redlining" is that some applicants are not evaluated on the basis of their individual creditworthiness. Rather, if they or their property has certain characteristics, the mortgage review process goes no further, and the application is denied. Those "code" characteristics—race, sex, or neighborhood—are used by the banker to stand for credit risk, even though a more thorough check might well show the borrower to be very creditworthy.

Even if the loan is not denied out of hand, at best, the borrower will have to put up with terms that do not directly correspond to his or her actual default risks. That is, even if prejudice does not completely preclude availability, it will increase cost.

The popular image of redlining pictures a mortgage banker drawing a circle around some neighborhood indicating that no home loans will be made there. The figurative line far more often excludes a type of borrower—the minority applicant—than a specific neighborhood, although this does occur as well (Shafer, 1978).

Why do financial institutions redline? Some redlining grows out of pure prejudice; an overwhelming white financial establishment confronting minorities with which it has had little contact in the past. But it also reflects an attempt to economize on information gathering and transaction costs.

Mortgage applicant characteristics and property location can be used as an early stage screen to filter out borrowers who would likely not qualify for mortgages if they or their proposed property acquisition received closer scrutiny. This so-called statistical discrimination saves the lender the added information costs of such an investigation.

Similarly, the lender knows that certain mortgages may be more expensive to service. For example, mortgages in an economically depressed neighborhood will tend to be relatively small in dollar terms, but the lender's costs in monitoring payment will be fairly constant across mortgage size, so that monitoring costs per dollar of funds loaned will be higher. Financial institutions often do not (and sometimes cannot) pass these costs on to the borrower. Instead they indiscriminately refuse to lend to any house buyers in the area.

Why they do not instead raise interest rates on certain mortgages to reflect higher information or transaction costs or higher risk is not well understood. As is often the case with young, small enterprises, when given a choice between raising rates to cover higher risks and costs, and not making the loan at all, bankers often take the easy way out. In some instances they are prevented from making the higher return by usury laws, as we shall discuss below.

To be effective, an anti-redlining law must take into account these diverse causes of redlining. Of equal importance, it must provide sanctions that will be sufficiently powerful to eliminate any *perceived* benefits of redlining. Recent state regulations appear to do a better job at the first task than the second one.

State regulations on mortgage lending have been targeted at both pure discrimination and statistical discrimination. Those regulations directed at pure discrimination, like Massachusetts' Fair Lending Law, simply put a total ban on the use of the borrower's race or sex as a lending criterion. This prohibition also means that these characteristics cannot be used as credit screens in the statistical discrimination process. The California Financial Discrimination Law (1977) extends the personal characteristic list to include religion, marital status, or ethnicity as well.

Regulations directed at statistical screens *other than* personal characteristics like those enumerated above must be more sophisticated. Greater sophistication is necessary because use of any of these other measures is not necessarily improper, but needs to be limited to cases where it has a demonstrably negative effect on the risk or cost of the transaction to the lender. For example, in California's law, neighborhood or geographic location of the real estate cannot be considered "unless the financial institution can demonstrate that such consideration in the particular case is required to avoid an unsafe or unsound business practice." Similarly, Michigan's statute specifies that "the age of the subject property or of other properties in the neighborhood cannot be used as a lending criterion, except as it directly relates to the physical condition and probable remaining useful life of the structure and nearby ones affecting the value of the property as collateral."

As an alternative to new statutes that prohibit discriminatory lending behavior, states can issue new regulatory interpretations of existing statutes. In Massachusetts, from 1974 to 1978, the state Board of Bank Incorporation took into account lending patterns in determining whether banks had met the statutory requirement that they serve the "convenience and needs" of the communities in which they operated. Virtually every state has such a "convenience and needs" standard in its laws governing state-chartered financial institutions; but seldom have they been used to influence lending behavior. Instead, they had traditionally been interpreted as only requiring that residents had a safe place to put their money, not borrow. In other words, regulations have tended to be concerned about monitoring the safety of deposits and not their use. On the other hand, when in 1975 the John Eliot Savings Bank petitioned the Massachusetts Banking Commission to pull out of black Roxbury, the petition was denied on grounds of failing to meet the "convenience and borrowing needs" of the community. In 1977, when the same bank petitioned to branch out to the suburbs, it was only granted approval when it agreed to a specific schedule of loan targets it would meet in Roxbury.

On the federal level, the Community Reinvestment Act of 1977 establishes the broader asset interpretation for use in regulation of financial institutions. In fact, it statutorily institutionalizes the regulatory standards developed in Massachusetts. New charters, new branches, and the closing of old branches will not be permitted unless they are found to meet the convenience and *credit* needs of the community served.

Establishing a statute or issuing a regulation mandating that lenders do not arbitrarily deny mortgage application or impose discriminatory terms is relatively easy, if seldom done. Incorporating penalties that will ensure compliance with these standards and monitoring the responsiveness of financial institutions is another matter. State regulations have usually taken one of three enforcement routes. In most states individual mortgage loan applicants who believe they have been treated improperly must initiate action. For example, under regulations like those in New Jersey the injured party can bring civil suit in the court system. Other states, such as Michigan, set up a special administrative apparatus, the mortgage review board. Lending institutions in a locality have the option to create voluntarily a board that will review complaints and place loans for applicants who have been improperly rejected. If the banks do not voluntarily establish one, or the review board established does not effectively resolve complaints, then the state can set up a mandatory review board. In addition, injured parties may bring civil suit, and institutions may be fined up to $10,000.

Going beyond this judicial and administrative redress for individual borrowers, California's anti-redlining statute introduces a third enforcement mechanism: "other provisions of law" governing state supervision of financial institutions. Broadly interpreted, this would statutorily include the regulatory power to deny branching or merger applications administratively adopted in Massachusetts and incorporated in the federal Community Reinvestment Act.

In practice, enforcement through individual civil suit or complaint to a review board is likely not to be very effective. Although lenders must inform each mortgage applicant of his or her rights, and provide written explanation of credit denial or variation in mortgage terms, financial institutions are in a position to manipulate information and camouflage the real basis of their decisions. Judicial remedies, when sought, will come to pass slowly, and penalties may be insignificant from the bank's (or savings and loan's) perspective. Consider, for example, the comparable record of judicial remedies in enforcing state anti-pollution laws. The mortgage review board represents a more immediate arena of appeal but can only assist individual casualties of improper mortgage lending practices and cannot apply any general sanctions against the offending institution.

California's mechanism is exceptional (and perhaps a model) in that the view of individual complaints can take place within the state supervisory agency, the Department of Business and Transportation. Its secretary can order the financial institution to make the mortgage loan, if it has been found in violation, or if that is no longer relevant, can impose a fine of up to $1,000 per violation. With this arrangement, penalties and remedial action are likely to be swifter, more certain and more frequent.

Yet these sanctions all seem inadequate where redlining is an entrenched practice and lenders see it as in their interest. At a minimum the state government, as opposed to individual citizens, should be able to initiate action against discriminating lenders on the basis of its ongoing monitoring of credit granting patterns. The most obvious penalty that regulators should have to exert pressure on intermediaries is the power to deny branching and merger applications. As the John Eliot Savings Bank case illustrates, this can put a serious crimp in the growth of a bank or savings and loan institution which does not comply.

For any anti-redlining regulatory process to work, there must be access to detailed information on the behavior of credit granting institutions. Accordingly, a major component of recent regulations has been a disclosure requirement. Regulation C of the Federal Home Mortgage Disclosure Act (1975) already requires reporting the number and total dollar amount of mortgage and home improvement loans originated or purchased by the lender during the preceding fiscal year, by census tract or ZIP code. However, this information simply will not suffice for diagnosing the existence of housing finance market imperfections.

To detect redlining, regulators need to be able to measure the relationship between a lender's rejection/acceptance decisions for mortgage credit and a host of borrower and property characteristics. Systematic discrimination will be evidenced through the statistical significance of certain suspect variables. Necessary information would include whether the loan was granted and if so, with what terms, the race, sex, marital status, age and credit background of the applicant; and the location, age and condition of the mortgaged property.

Virtually all of this information is now available to federal regulators through Federal Home Loan Bank Board (savings and loans) and Federal Deposit Insurance Corporation requirements. However, our federal system requires that state governments must acquire this information on their own. They may simply, however, require that each institution make identical reports available to them. Their right to do so with regard to state-chartered financial institutions is clear, but their power to obtain it from federally chartered ones is more ambiguous (see Johnson, 1978).

Given what we know of the pitfalls of financial market regulation from earlier chapters, the obstacles to designing and implementing effective anti-redlining codes fit into the "two horns of a dilemma" pattern we have seen. Regulation which is too lax or which concentrates too much on the safety of liabilities and not enough on the use of assets will not sufficiently encourage more risk taking on the part of lenders. Regulation which tries to force lenders to lend where the risks are too great in relation to the return will act as a tax, and may drive essential capital assets out of state.

State regulators must, on the one hand, require lenders to go beyond typical prejudicial early stage screening criteria, but at the same time permit them to vary mortgage terms and interest rates in response to actual differences in risk producing characteristics. They must bring forth the information needed for determining who is redlining, and who is not. And they must provide a sanction powerful enough to outweigh any perceived benefits of improper discrimination. Finally, new state anti-redlining regulatory initiatives must be especially good in order to justify themselves, since a whole range of like-minded statutes already exist at the federal level. These include the Fair Housing Act (1968, amended 1974), the Equal Credit Opportunity Act (1974, amended 1976), and the Community Reinvestment Act (CRA) (1977).

Even where government action is effective, the spectre of retaliation by financial institutions exists. Banks may stop branch operation entirely or not establish ones in areas where redlining might normally be practiced, to avoid being forced to make mortgage loans they would otherwise deny. Fortunately, this response seems less likely in the case of anti-redlining regulations as compared to other ones that attempt to mandate lending behavior. Because these rules do not require that truly unsound loans be made, the added risks they impose on lenders are largely perceived risks, not actual ones. Moreover, the most sophisticated regulations, like the CRA, make the wholesale closing down of a branch to avoid alteration of past, improper lending practices itself punishable.

Floating usury ceilings: Ceilings on the interest rates that lenders can charge for mortgage credit evolved to protect both the general borrowing public from monopolistic financial institutions and the unsophisticated borrower from exploitation. When nominal interest rates lay at their traditional level during the earlier non-inflationary decades of this century, such usury ceilings only blocked loans that would have been made on extraordinarily unfavorable terms from the borrower's perspective. They did not stand in the way of normal mortgages made in competitive markets. But exceptionally high market interest rates accompanying periods of high inflation this decade have made usury ceilings a serious barrier to the availability of mortgage credit.

In the 15 states with fixed ceilings of 10 percent or less, lenders have not always been able to charge an interest rate that would make a mortgage loan competitive with other investments. As a consequence, either the institutions themselves channel funds into open market securities rather than usury ceiling-bound home mortgages, or their individual depositors do so on their own.

This situation particularly hurts the less favored mortgage applicant. For a financial institution to provide mortgage credit to an applicant who is riskier or more expensive to deal with, it must be able to charge a relatively higher interest rate. So interest rate caps first become constraining for the more seriously disadvantaged people. One study found that the costs of usury ceilings is borne primarily by young, low-to-moderate income households entering the home buying market for the first time. As many as 80 percent of the first time home buyers will be unable to obtain the necessary mortgage credit. Lenders unable to raise interest rates compensate by reducing the risk of mortgage loans they make. They do so by requiring higher downpayments, which these same young, low-to-moderate income applicants cannot pay (Parliment and Koden, 1979).

Several states have gone to the heart of the problem and reformed their usury laws. This has been accomplished in one of three ways: eliminating the ceiling outright; setting it at a new, higher level; or tying it to the general level of market interest rates.

Scrapping the ceilings altogether has not been attractive since many constituencies believe that the regulations are still needed to protect the consumer, even if they are adjusted upward to reflect current financial market realities.

Adopting an inflated ceiling relieves the immediate pressure, but unless it is substantially raised, it creates the possibility of renewed difficulties should inflation become even more virulent. For example, Arizona adopted a new fixed ceiling of 12 percent in September, 1978, but as interest rates continue to shoot up, this previously high rate already has become a constraint on mortgage lending. Yet if ceilings are set too high, then their perceived value for consumer protection will vanish.

The compromise between usury ceiling elimination and new, fixed rates is the floating usury ceiling now found in ten states. Key choices in implementing this approach involve the index that the floating ceiling will be pegged to, as well as the differential that will be allowed. Six states peg it at from 1.5 percent to 2.5 percent over the monthly index of long-term U.S. government bond yields. Four states peg it from 3.0 percent to 5.0 percent over an index of lower, short-term rates.

However, these differentials may not be generous enough since mortgage rates normally sit well above these indices. For example, the spread between mortgage rates and long-term U.S. bonds from 1974 to 1979 was over 2.0 percent during nearly half that time. So the allowable gap between an index and the ceiling must be large enough to include this spread, as well as the possible added interest rate premium lenders must charge on riskier or higher information/transaction cost mortgages. The best solution may be to use conventional mortgage rates established in the large, national secondary market as the base index and then allow premiums of up to at least 1.0 percent to 1.5 percent beyond that (Parliment and Koden, 1979).

Variable rate mortgages: Besides placing a ceiling on mortgage interest rates, most state governments have discouraged lenders from offering variable rate mortgages (VRMs). This type of mortgage, as distinct from the traditional fixed payment one (FPM) allows for adjustment of its interest rate as market interest rates change. The VRM can generally help increase the availability of mortgage loans, as has now been recognized by a handful of states and the Federal Home Loan Bank Board.

The Variable Rate Mortgage (VRM) guarantees that the lending institution will be getting a high enough interest return from its mortgage assets to attract deposits by paying out a competitive interest rate. Fixed Payment Mortgages (FPMs) lock the financial intermediary into an interest return that may not keep up with volatile market interest rates. This results in the institution not being able to pay a deposit interest rate sufficient to get funds needed to make new mortgage loans. Since barriers to competition for deposits between mortgage lenders and other financial markets are being broken down, it becomes increasingly important that these institutions be able to pay competitive rates.

In economic terms, the variable rate mortgage permits the risk of rising interest rates to be shared between the lender and the borrower, as opposed to it all being on the lender. This makes sense in terms of our public policy concern to increase the overall availability of funds for mortgage lending. But how does it work for the individual home owner who gets the variable rate mortgage? The disadvantage of possible mortgage payment increases is obvious.

On the positive side, the interest rate on a new VRM will be lower than the rate on an FPM. This advantage exists because FPM lenders must charge a higher initial interest rate to cover themselves in the event that market interest rates rise during the life of the mortgage. In those New England states which permit VRMs, the difference is ½ percent; in California is ¼ percent.

In addition to this discount, VRM borrowers usually get certain guarantees governing how much their mortgage rate can rise in the future. For example, in California state-chartered savings and loans that originate VRMs cannot raise the interest rate more than 2½ percent cumulatively. Moreover, rate adjustments can only happen if an index of the average cost of funds to state savings and loans changes. Within these bounds, rate *increases* are at the option of the lender, while rate *decreases* are mandatory.

The ultimate safeguard to the borrower is his or her right to prepay the mortgage before it matures by refinancing the home through another lender. This ensures that a VRM interest rate will not rise above the prevailing mortgage rates at any time. Thus many VRM lenders in California and other states have not raised their rates even when legally permitted because they would have been higher than, or close to, the rates on new mortgages.

As of July 1, 1979, all federally chartered S&Ls will be able to issue variable rate mortgages because of a new Federal Home Loan Bank Board ruling. These institutions will join lenders in California, Ohio, Wisconsin, Maine, New Hampshire and Connecticut which have already been given this option by their respective state governments (Melton and Heidt, 1979).

Economic Incentives A handful of state governments have attempted to influence the flow of private home mortgage funds through reducing the risk lenders must assume in making such loans. State housing agencies in states like Maryland, Connecticut, Vermont and Alaska achieve this goal through home mortgage loan guarantee programs they operate.

The basic model for this mechanism is provided by the Maryland Housing Fund program under the state's Department of Economic and Community Development. Any home buyers who cannot obtain uninsured mortgages in their area are eligible for the Fund's guarantee service. It will insure up to 25 percent of a mortgage, and charges the borrower a premium for this commitment. The initial reserve fund to back the guarantee program came from a $7 million general obligation bond issue, but it is now self-supporting (Bureau of National Affairs, 1977).

The Alaska Housing Finance Corporation (AHFC) is the fourth largest financial intermediary in Alaska, with assets of over $200 million. Until 1975, its secondary marketing operation was limited to federally issued FHA or VA loans, the requisite for both of which was often inappropriate to Alaska's economy and population, particularly in small, outlying rural areas. Thus in 1975, AHFC established its own mortgage insurance program. Contrary to expectations, this new tool has not appreciably changed AHFC's risk mix. The portfolio is still essentially composed of loans to white, middle-income residents of Anchorage, not rural Native Alaskans.

Direct State Intermediation While state agencies that raise capital for housing development have been around since New York's pioneering effort in 1961, until the early 1970's they were almost exclusively tools for indirectly subsidizing multi-family housing. Only more recently did the 34 state housing finance agencies (HFAs) begin using their resources to overcome imperfections in the home mortgage market that deny funds to creditworthy borrowers. Perhaps the initial move in this direction came in 1974 with Virginia's issuing the first HFA tax-exempt bonds to raise money for single family home mortgage lending. By 1978, 62 percent of all capital raised by state HFA's—$2.8 billion—went for this type of financing (Smith, 1979). Unfortunately, much of this capital has gone toward mortgage loans that private financial institutions would have made in the absence of HFAs, thus failing to make its way to borrowers who have been unreasonably discriminated against and who cannot get access to mortgage loans.

The obstacles to a successful bond-financed state home mortgage intermediary mirror those barriers to an effective bond-financed state business loan intermediary discussed in the last chapter. Like their business financing relatives, HFAs primarily rely on revenue bonds to raise capital. Since they are secured only by the repayment of mortgage principal and interest, these bonds tend to be marketable only if investors believe they are being used to finance home buyers the private market would normally find bankable. As the chairman of the Federal Home Bank Board, Robert McKinney, has stated, "The people who market these bonds want the highest income bracket possible in order to get the highest rating and make the bonds saleable" (Glen, 1979).

Besides being constrained by the manner in which they raise capital, HFAs have also had problems due to the mechanisms they rely upon for channeling this money to home mortgage borrowers. The funds have been used either to make loans to home mortgage lenders, who in turn use the money to make mortgage loans, or to purchase a dominant interest in mortgages originated by private lenders. Although the HFA can specify criteria that private lenders must use if their mortgages are to qualify for either of these programs, it remains likely that these financial institutions will retain their normal lending practices whenever possible. In contrast, bond-financed state business loan intermediaries usually deal directly with borrowers, not tying themselves to the discriminatory filtering process of private lenders.

Not only do HFA operations suffer from some of the same structural constraints as business financing programs, they also may incorporate some of the same faulty assumptions about the cost of capital as an attractive device. Here the targets are not footloose corporations, but middle-income home buyers trying to decide whether to live in the central city or a suburban area. Mortgage loans become a vehicle for subsidy in reduced interest costs to buyers willing to locate in the central city. The subsidy, as in the case of the business loans, is the difference between the normal lending rate and the tax-exempt bond rate. It is indirectly paid by the federal government in lost tax revenues. Under early-1979 capital market conditions the borrower receiving tax-exempt bond financing gets an interest rate about 2.0 percent below the prevailing rate. He or she saves about 20 percent of the interest cost of buying a home. In contrast to a thirty year, $50,000 mortgage that would normally cost $457 a month in interest, only $371 must be paid.

No evidence has been offered to show that this subsidy represents a sufficient incentive to influence intrametropolitan residential location decisions. In fact there have been findings to the contrary (Verbruge, 1979). Based on what we know about the ineffectiveness of comparable industrial location incentives, combined with the observable insensitivity of recent home mortgage demand to rapidly rising interest rates, it would be surprising if these subsidies had much impact. This is true even though capital costs are more important in housing than business development. However, subsidies do impose definite costs. Beyond the lost opportunity to help solve mortgage market imperfections, the rising use of tax-exempt single family mortgage bonds will raise state and local borrowing costs across the board. One analyst has estimated that if $13 billion of these bonds (a not unreasonable amount in the near future) were issued in 1979, all tax-exempt interest rates would be driven up nearly 1 percent (Smith, 1979).

The use of tax-exempt single family housing bonds has proliferated most recently at the local level in those thirteen states that permit their localities to issue such bonds. Moreover, it is at the local level that mortgages financed by these bonds have been most poorly targeted. Municipalities often place no income ceiling on which families will be eligible for the special mortgage financing, or set the cut-off so high, say at $40,000, they effectively allow in almost anyone. In response, the federal government has moved to put a brake on use of the bonds. Proposals now being entertained in Congress range from a total cut-off on these bond issues to a requirement that the proceeds only be used to finance mortgages that otherwise could not be obtained.

PUBLIC INFRASTRUCTURE FINANCING

As one of the least organized sectors of the American capital market, the submarkets for local governmental debt stand ripe for intervention. Already several states have recognized and taken advantage of this opportunity for improving the capacity of their counties and cities to raise capital. Their approaches to increasing market efficiency span all three mechanisms for state intervention in capital markets. They illustrate how state governments can make capital availability and cost to localities actually mirror those jurisdictions' ability to repay rather than reflecting breakdowns in financial intermediation.

Administrative Regulations

When the federal government began regulating corporate securities in 1933 with the establishment of the SEC Act, it specifically exempted state and local bonds from the new procedures. This has left a large gap in the regulation of the tax-exempt bond market that continually creates problems for local government bond issues. In particular, the absence of registration and disclosure requirements has meant a dearth of trustworthy and easily acquirable information for prospective suppliers of funds.

As a prerequisite for later disclosure, local government units must maintain sound information about their financial condition. Currently, uniform or reliable accounting practices among municipalities which bond buyers need in order to evaluate creditworthiness generally does not exist. If it exists at all, it cannot be easily interpreted because of idiosyncratic record keeping.

By mandating a standard accounting procedure for its local governments, a state can assure the availability of information necessary for disclosure and investor monitoring of municipal and county borrowers. In fourteen states standard accounting procedures have been made mandatory, and another twenty-nine states encourage voluntary compliance through issuing standard procedures (Coe, 1978).

A complete accounting process must provide for not only record-keeping procedures, but auditing as well. That is, promised performance must be reviewed to see if records have been properly maintained and accurately portray the financial situation. Thirty states require such annual post audits, and twenty-five actually perform field audit reviews of localities.

The first step in developing mandatory accounting and auditing procedures is designing a uniform system. Many but not all states with regulations use the "generally accepted accounting system" and "generally accepted auditing system" as models. Those states that do not will reduce the value of their efforts. Since the need for information is not entirely uniform across all sizes of localities, regulations can and do differ for size and type of government unit. Penalties for non-compliance also need to be established; they typically include removal from office of responsible officials and the cutoff of state aid to the locality (Petersen, et al., 1977). In general, state regulation of local accounting and auditing practices accomplishes its immediate purpose. A recent study (University of Georgia, 1978) found a direct observable relationship between the degree of state control and the efficiency of financial management in cities with populations under 50,000.

While requiring the keeping of sound financial accounts at the local level is a prerequisite for public disclosure, it will not guarantee it. Rather, the state must perform two additional tasks. First, it should have the power to approve or reject local bond sales on the basis of compliance with disclosure requirements. Second, the state should on its own *collect* information from local governments, maintain central data files and disseminate it. Thus investors will have an alternative, ongoing source of information on their public debtors.

While forty-one states currently have agencies that supervise local borrowing or gather information, their actual authority varies greatly. Less than half (19) perform some kind of review function, and only nine have the power to explicitly approve or reject bond offerings. A total of fourteen states can prescribe the contents of the official statements accompanying local bond issues, a crucial power for regulating disclosure (Petersen, et al., 1977).

Almost all states collect financial data on local government units. But the coverage of this information and methods of dissemination differ. Usually information on tax revenue and debt is collected, but more general economic and demographic information is only routinely compiled by thirteen states. In thirty-six states the data is regularly published, while in fourteen it is available only on request.

State governmental regulation of local borrowing appears to really make a difference in local access to capital. In North Carolina, the state with the most comprehensive system of supervision, localities have higher credit ratings, get more bids for their bonds and pay lower interest rates than ones in comparable states. These interest savings have been estimated at from .3 percent to 1.0 percent, depending on the methodology used. One researcher found that, in general, state supervision of local financial management and bond sales "will improve investors' rankings of a community's credit quality in relation to other borrowers. Furthermore, the degree of improvement in rankings desired from such assistance is greater, the lower the credit quality and the smaller the size of the governmental unit (Petersen, 1977).

Economic Incentives Stricter regulation of local government financial practices addresses the sufficiency of information to bond rating agencies and private investors involved in evaluating a community's creditworthiness. A key alternative would be to remove these actors from the risk assessing and bearing process entirely and instead, substitute a state government agency. In a handful of states this is exactly what is done through the mechanisms of muncipal bond guarantee programs.

In principle, state municipal bond guarantee programs operate just like state business loan guarantee programs. The state government commits itself to cover some portion of debt service payments on public debt should local funds be insufficient. Not surprisingly, the same issues we confronted in designing a business loan guarantee program in Chapter 5 arise again with regard to municipal bond guarantees: who should be eligible, what percentage of an issue should be insured, how large a premium should be charged, and what type of security need be offered (Minge, 1974)?

Targeting who is eligible varies from state to state. The broadest approach has been taken in Minnesota, where the Bond Guarantee Fund started in 1971 can insure any general obligation bond issue of a political subdivision in the state. In other states the insurance has been limited to narrower classes of public infrastructure projects. In California, the Health Facility Construction Loan Insurance program can guarantee revenue or general obligation bonds of health facilities being developed in accordance with state health plans. Both New

Hampshire and Michigan have the capacity to insure school district bonds, and New Hampshire guarantees revenue or general obligation bonds for sewage and pollution control facilities as well.

In limiting itself to guaranteeing g.o. bonds, the Minnesota program neglects the less secured revenue bonds that are likely to confront the most problems in marketability. However, unlike the major private municipal bond insurer, the American Municipal Bond Assurance Corporation (AMBAC), the state does not screen out bonds that would be rated below medium grade, or issues of either very small or very large size.

Existing municipal bond guarantee programs do not have all the characteristics that a well-designed market perfecting program would possess. Unlike most state business loan guarantee programs, they typically insure 100 percent of a bond issue. The exception is the New Hampshire school bond program. Clearly this gives no incentive for private bond buyers to do any in depth evaluation of creditworthiness. It places a great deal of responsibility on the state agency administering the program. Moreover, only the Minnesota and California insurance programs charge fees even approaching the actuarially based default costs of insured bonds. The other ones charge fees only covering administrative costs. And in the two states that do collect a risk premium, it does not vary with the underlying riskiness of the guaranteed bonds. Minnesota has a flat fee equal to 2½ percent of the principal or $1,000, whichever is higher. In California the fee cannot exceed 1/2 percent of the principal outstanding in any one year and is payable annually. In contrast to these public insurance programs, AMBAC separately evaluates the quality of each issue it insures; based on this assessment it charges a sliding premium.

Moreover, each program offers security for its guarantee that it tends to be excessive when measured against what an efficient market would require. In Minnesota the first line of defense in case of a default is the proceeds of guarantee fees that have accumulated in a reserve fund. If this does not suffice, the state must sell up to $20 million in bonds to cover defaults. Minnesota cannot insure an aggregate amount of bond greater than 20 times this money in or available to the reserve fund. In addition to these safeguards, the state may levy a special property tax on the locality in default to later recover any money it had to pay out. In California there is similarly a loan insurance fund consisting of paid-in guarantee fees, but they are ultimately backed by the *full* faith and credit of the state.

The programs have been at least partially successful. Ideally, a guaranteed bond would be perceived as so risk free that the obligatory rating from Standard and Poor's or Moody's would not have to be sought. But the guaranteed bond issues have still felt it necessary to obtain a rating. As one might expect, Standard and Poor's has viewed the guarantees as strong protection for the investor, giving an automatic AA rating (the second highest) to an issuer insured by the Minnesota, California and Michigan programs and a top AAA for those insured by New Hampshire. Moody's claims it treats a guarantee more cautiously and critically, but has consistently given high ratings to state guaranteed bonds, comparable to those given by Standard and Poor's. Thus, municipal bond issues that otherwise would have received a medium or lower rating clearly gain a higher rating and consequent reduced interest cost when covered by a state guarantee.

Even though existing state guarantees reduce interest costs for localities, this is not necessarily evidence that these programs actually improve market efficiency. One would need to see that the sum of post-guarantee interest costs *and* the accurate risk premium paid for participation in the program was less than interest costs for a similar issue without a guarantee. Since existing state programs in practice undercharge or overcharge for their risk premiums or fees, this cannot be ascertained. In addition, it would be important to know whether the guarantees have made bonds marketable that were completely unmarketable otherwise.

Direct State Intermediation

Even with a municipal bond guarantee, local governments still face many problems involved in dealing directly with the capital market. For example. small issues must still absorb substantial fixed transaction costs when they market a bond issue. To help their political subdivisions overcome these obstacles, state governments can take the added step of creating specialized financial intermediaries that will go to the capital market for them. First started in Vermont during 1970, state municipal bond banks have since been initiated in Maine, Alaska and North Dakota.

In the basic municipal bond bank model developed in Maine and Vermont, the process of raising capital for local communities consists of four major steps. First, the bank determines which governmental units want to borrow through it and how much they need to raise. Next, it screens out any muncipalities whose participation in the consolidated borrowing of the bank would jeopardize the issue's perceived creditworthiness. The bond bank then issues its own bonds in an amount equal to the total borrowing needs of the local communities plus 10 percent that will be put in a reserve fund to serve as security for the issue. Finally, the bank uses the capital raised to buy the general obligation bonds of the participating local government units.

The market-perfecting impacts of a municipal bond bank are threefold. First, consolidation of several smaller issues into one large issue reduces overall transaction costs. Relatively fixed charges for bond counsel, printing, and underwriting get spread over several borrowing communities, lowering the expense each locality must incur. Second, the bond bank economizes on the total information gathering costs that would be involved in several smaller, separate bond issues. The bank stands close to the borrowing local governments and can investigate their creditworthiness easier than an investor at large. Third, the packaging of individual local issues into one bond bank issue may provide some otherwise unavailable opportunities for risk diversification to investors. Both the information availability and risk pooling market perfections would show up in a higher credit rating and lower interest rate for the bond bank's debt as compared to how the local bond issues would have been treated individually. It could also show up in the *availability* of funds to a locality that simply could not afford to borrow at all in the absence of the bond bank.

Interpreting the market perfecting performance of the Maine and Vermont type municipal bond bank is difficult. Clearly it reduces transaction costs. For example, the overhead for the Vermont bank's first issue in 1970 was one-half of what it would have been had the participating communities raised the same amount of capital on their own.

The institution's influence on improving risk assessment and bearing is more ambiguous. Bond buyers and rating agencies have rated the bond bank issues highly, and this has meant interest rate savings for the local government borrowers averaging .4 percent to .5 percent. But some portion of the reduced risk premiums reflect the fact that the state has put additional security behind the consolidated bond issue. First, there is the reserve fund it sets up equal to 10 percent of the amount borrowed by the bond governments. Second, the state has made a moral obligation to make up deficiencies in the reserve fund out of its general revenues. These forms of security are in addition to the basic collateral of the bank being able to take a lien on property in a defaulting jurisdiction. Since the state does not charge local borrowers for the risk it bears in putting up these additional forms of security, it is impossible to determine if the interest savings the localities receive represents a true improvement in risk assessment and pooling, or a hidden subsidy from the state.

Municipal bond banks will make their greatest contribution in states like Maine and Vermont, where localities are small in size. Over 90 percent of the cities and towns in these two states formerly sold bonds that were not rated at all. In states where larger communities predominate, the impact of this type of institution will be proportionately smaller, but still may well justify the effort.

TARGETING CAPITAL TO COMMUNITIES

Economic development is uneven within states, just as it differs between them. Consider the economy of one large South Atlantic state. Between 1970 and 1977 total employment there increased by 8.5 percent. But during this same period total employment in the thirty municipalities considered the most economically disadvantaged grew by a paltry amount, less than one percent. Similarly, per capita money income statewide rose by 30 percent between 1970 and 1975. But in those distressed communities it increased by only 23 percent, making them relatively less well off than before.

In Northeastern and North Central states, the most striking unevenness tends to be between central cities and suburbs in metropolitan areas. In the Southeast and South Central states, the gap is typically between the better off metropolitan areas and the worse off rural areas and small towns.

Regardless of how it manifests itself, the existence of relatively depressed communities in substate regions means a certain segment of the population may be largely cut off from the fruits of state economic development. People in these locales will not simply migrate to the healthier areas, thereby solving the problem. On the contrary, surveys that trace the status of individuals over time show that it is the younger, better educated people, with more promising job prospects to start with, who are likely to move from place to place looking for employment. Moves by poor people tend to be within the same county or city. Clearly there is a need to try to bring jobs to people, rather than just counting on people to move to the jobs.

Given the need to give a greater push to development in some places as opposed to others, how can a state government employ capital-related policies to help out? Generally, the principles of development finance we have laid out in previous chapters can be applied to substate development problems with certain modifications. Most importantly, the caveats apply. Just as supplying capital statewide will not necessarily lead to more investment, more jobs and greater incomes, boosting the supply of capital in a depressed substate region will not necessarily benefit that area. The reason is the same: factors other than the cost and availability of capital typically determine the level of investment in any area. These factors include the area's proximity to markets and the local cost of labor, land, energy and other requisites of production. Rather than being depressed because of the relatively high cost of obtaining funds or geographic limits on the potential availability of capital, these locations are primarily disadvantaged with respect to the other factors that influence business profitability.

However, just as capital-related policies could play a role in promoting statewide economic development in spite of these realities, they can contribute to aiding depressed substate areas as well. While the unavailability of capital for viable enterprises does not account for the basic plight of depressed areas, these places do contain *some* opportunities for business, housing and infrastructure developing possessing all the necessary ingredients for success except for capital. Thus policies designed to solve capital market imperfections statewide will also enhance the prospects of these underfunded ventures in depressed areas. For example, anti-redlining programs will increase home mortgage loans in central cities, and anti-monopoly banking programs will increase business loans in rural areas suffering from poverty.

Although the undirected workings of such statewide programs may help out poor or declining communities, they will not provide much differential assistance. How can capital-related policies be used to give more concentrated aid?

In general, there are two alternatives that a state can think about. First, regardless of how desirable solving capital market imperfections may be, no state will have unlimited resources for ensuring that capital is being made available to the most productive enterprises. If a state government wants to give an extra push to development in depressed areas, it can give priority to solving the problem of competitive but capital poor projects in these communities. In essence, it will be rationing market-perfecting intervention on the basis of need. A positive side-effect of this approach may be the attraction of entrepreneurial talent to depressed areas as a result of the differential availability of capital there; this will be in addition to the stimulation of indigenous ventures.

Second, a subsidy delivered through a below market cost of capital can be used to compensate enterprises for the added costs of operating in a depressed area. These firms may be already located in the area, or considering moving or starting up there. We have taken a guarded view of such capital subsidies when used to promote statewide economic development, and will offer some of the same criticisms of their use in aiding substate regions. Nevertheless, it should be entertained as one tool in the development finance kit for restricted use.

GEOGRAPHICALLY TARGETING CAPITAL AVAILABILITY FOR UNDERFINANCED ENTERPRISES

Any of the capital market-perfecting policies discussed in previous chapters can be applied exclusively, or at least with priority, to poor or declining communities. This targeting has been rare in the case of regulatory interventions. It has been more common, but still rare, in the case of guarantee programs and direct public financial intermediation.

The outstanding model of a program that targets capital availability for underfinanced businesses to a substate depressed area is the Kentucky Highlands Investment Corporation, introduced in Chapter 6. Nearly a decade old, KHIC is a non-profit community development corporation funded by the federal Community Services Administration. The organization operates and makes investments in a classically depressed nine county non-metropolitan area in southeastern Kentucky. Its 180,000 people almost all live in communities of 300 or less. Unemployment has been estimated at 21.9 percent when "discouraged" job-hunters are included. The 1978 median income was $5,878 as compared to $11,200 statewide and $14,900 in the United States as a whole.

Although the dollars it receives from the federal government come in the form of grants that do not have to be repaid, the investments KHIC makes are at market rates. That the organization has been able to identify and develop business opportunities in the area that appear able to produce the necessary market return represents KHIC's most important lesson.

The eleven small companies in which KHIC has made major investments all illustrate that even a southeastern Kentucky—with its distance from markets and suppliers and lack of skilled and experienced labor—can nourish certain kinds of enterprises. Outdoor Venture Corporation began in 1973 and now employs 180 people with sales of $8.1 million as of 1977. OVC manufactures family camping tents. Possum Trot Corporation, KHIC's first venture and a manufacturer of soft toys, had sales of $1.1 million and employed 100 people by 1977. The other firms KHIC has helped to start or expand include:

> Phoenix Products, Inc., now the largest kayak producer in the country; Kentucky Woodcrafts Inc., a manufacturer of hardwood trophy bases and plaques; Williamsburg Hog Enterprises, a hog fattening operation that feeds 5,000 hogs annually; American Bag Corp., a subsidiary of Outdoor Venture Corporation that manufactures sleeping bags; Kirby Steel Products Inc., a manufacturer of coal truck beds and truck body accessories; L&R Farm Inc., a high-volume, enclosed hog feedlot operation, Rockcastle Steel Corporation, a fabricator of structural steel

for the construction and coal industries; Hanna Sand and Gravel Corp., a quarrying operation; and a uniform manufacturing plant subsidiary of the Cintas Corp., a Cincinnati-based uniform rental company. (Pierce and Hagstrom, 1979)

Kentucky Highlands has invested $3.09 million in these ventures, whose total assets stand in excess of $10 million. Thus it has leveraged over $3 from private sources for every $1 it has committed. The only loss has been a $47,000 loan made in 1973 to a feeder pig operation.

An ability to identify and attract good entrepreneurs with sound business plans has been the single most crucial element in its success. In turn, this ability is largely based on the one thing available in southeastern Kentucky not typically available in many other locations. As KHIC's director of business development puts it, "KHIC's main attraction is that we do have what is probably the rarest form of venture capital—seed capital for start-up and early-stage ventures involving little or no technology." The organization annually receives about 400 inquiries from people around the country with venture proposals. In addition, it has Venture Founders, Inc. (formerly the Institute for New Enterprise Development) of Belmont, Massachusetts on near constant retainer to scour the country for potential entrepreneurs. The few dozen most promising come to weekend workshops run by Venture Founders and KHIC where the best are filtered out. Continual technical assistance is provided to those enterprises that do get financed, and the organization sometimes exerts added control through a seat on the board of directors.

An urban counterpart of KHIC is the National Development Council (NDC), a non-profit organization that helps target capital availability for underfinanced small firms in central city areas around the country. NDC has a small staff of expert loan packagers that specializes in finding government and private long-term financing for growing small enterprises in distressed urban communities. While it does not have a direct source of capital, its loan packagers have managed to put together 426 deals totaling $151 million between 1970 and 1978. By skilled negotiation with all parties involved and a thorough knowledge of Small Business Administration and Economic Development Administration loan programs, NDC "greases the pipeline" through which capital flows from distant sources to local development. It is comparable to the "market makers" in other, more developed private capital markets that bring borrowers and lenders together though not supplying any funds themselves.

Like KHIC, NDC aids enterprises which do not need subsidies to survive and grow, yet are not being well served by conventional sources of capital. Of the loans it has been involved in, only 3 percent have defaulted. This indicates that the ventures have been overwhelmingly successful; but since it is well above the less than one percent default rate that commercial banks would normally find acceptable, it also shows NDC to be successful in freeing up funds for the riskier enterprises most in need of capital.

Take the case of ALDI Corporation, a fast growing machinery servicing company in San Diego that wanted to expand on a site within one of the city's minority neighborhoods. Unavailability of capital blocked this growth: a commercial bank would provide only 70 percent of the required $767,000 financing. According to the firm's president, "To raise the other 30 percent, I would have to sell my home, my wife, my kid, and I'd still be $10 short." But the city and NDC jointly put together a financing package that required him to only come up with $57,000 and the plant got built (*Business Week,* 7/17/78).

Not only does capital availability mean growth for enterprises that would otherwise stagnate, it also means retaining some firms that would otherwise move to the suburbs. Take the case of the O'Brien Corporation, a profitable but small plastics manufacturing business in the blue-collar Italian Hill district of St. Louis. The firm wanted to relocate in expanded facilities in the suburbs, but the bank demanded a loan term too short for the company's cash flow. Given alternative long-term financing arranged by the city and NDC if O'Brien stayed in the same neighborhood, the company decided its chances for successful growth were better in a vacant plant six blocks away than in the suburbs. St. Louis' director of economic development regards the NDC approach as "an extremely valuable tool in slowing down the outflow of small business."

The best example of a state level program that at least attempts to ration its capital availability according to the economic distress of its substate areas is the Pennsylvania Industrial Development Authority. In PIDA direct loan financings, a private financial institution must provide at least 50 percent of the capital, with PIDA and the local industrial development agency splitting responsibility for the remainder. The amount of PIDA maximum participation depends on the unemployment rate where the borrowing firm operates. As of 1976, it provided 30 percent when the unemployment rate was at least 4 percent, 40 percent when it was at least 6 percent, 45 percent when it was at least 8 percent, and 50 percent when it was 10 percent or more.

A much smaller program that also targets capital availability is the New Jersey Urban Loan Authority. Capitalized in 1971 with $2 million from the state treasury, it has built up a fund of $6 million by 1977. NJULA at first only served distressed cities, but has been expanded to deal with distressed rural areas as well. It first tries to get commercial bank financing for eligible firms using loan guarantees. If unsuccessful, the institution can loan up to $250,000 for as long as ten years.

COMPENSATING FOR LOCATIONAL DISADVANTAGES THROUGH CAPITAL SUBSIDIES

While state programs subsidizing business capital costs predominate throughout the country, these incentive devices are normally available uniformly within a state. That is, they have not been limited to depressed areas so as to specifically reduce their cost of production disadvantages. For example, a recent survey of state industrial revenue bond programs—the leading vehicle for providing capital at below market rates—found that "Industrial revenue financing programs that aim to create and preserve jobs are not targeted by states to areas of surplus labor and low income but rather generally can be used throughout a state" (IILED, 1979). Moreover, to the extent local initiative is involved in using a statewide program, it will often be the ascendant communities with staff resources that employ them most frequently.

There has been a similar failure in state housing finance efforts to effectively target capital subsidies to those communities most in need. More than three-fourths of the states have established HFAs. But, as documented by a McKinsey and Company study, 80 percent of HFA-produced housing is in the suburbs, and only 10 percent has gone to low income individuals (Bureau of National Affairs, 1979).

Even when a state does try to target a capital subsidy program, it may easily snag itself on the kind of obstacles that plague the statewide development subsidy programs criticized in Chapters 4 through 6. One recent study—of the Connecticut Urban Jobs Program—highlights many of these problems (Ujakovich, 1979).

In 1978 Connecticut began offering incentives to firms which expand employment within one of the state's "high unemployment" or "economically distressed" communities. In cities and towns with an unemployment rate of at least 110 percent of the state average and 6 percent for the preceding calendar year, expanding manufacturing firms are eligible for: (1) a one-time $500 grant for each new job created by the expansion; (2) reduction of one percentage point on the interest charges for direct state loans used to finance an expansion; and (3) elimination of the 1/2 percent interest charged for state mortgage guarantees. Economically distressed areas are cities and towns which meet the threshold levels of distress for the Federal Urban Development Action Grant program, including age of housing, per capita income, lag in population growth, lag in employment growth, unemployment and proportion of population in poverty. In these areas expanding manufacturing firms are eligible for: 1) an 80 percent tax abatement for five years on the local property tax on the expansion facility and machinery and equipment (the locality is reimbursed by state for 75 percent of the lost revenue); 2) a 25 percent reduction for ten years in the corporate income tax due to the expansion; 3) working capital loans of up to $75,000 for small businessmen; and 4) state aid to municipalities for the financing of mini-industrial parks. Forty of the state's 169 cities and towns have received high unemployment designation and eighteen have received distressed designation. Of the latter group, twelve are also high unemployment designees, and thus eligible for both sets of incentives.

Of the seven incentives in the package, three can be thought of as reducing the costs of capital expenditures. The capital subsidies consist of low interest loans, the elimination of the guarantee charge, and the abatement of taxes on capital assets. The job grant is a wage subsidy, the corporate income tax reduction a general costs of production subsidy, the mini-industrial parks a land subsidy, and the working capital loans a potential market-correcting policy of the type discussed in the last section.

To what extent does this package of incentives compensate a firm for the higher costs of production involved in operating in a high unemployment or economically distressed community? The Ujakovich study estimated the present value of investment and operating costs for typical firms over a ten year period in urban, suburban and rural Connecticut locations. Reductions in these costs due to the combined incentives package as well as the separate high unemployment and economic distress packages were also estimated. The costs accounted for in these estimates include building, equipment, land labor, property taxes and business income taxes. They do not include transportation costs for inputs or products.

The high unemployment area incentives appear to be inadequate to offset the cost disadvantages of an urban location within the state. They reduce costs by about 1 percent. In comparison, urban location costs in Connecticut are 1 percent to 5 percent greater than suburban costs. Moreover, this does not take into consideration that many Connecticut cities have very congested transportation systems, nor does it allow for the practical problems of urban land assembly and the twice higher crime rates. The potential of high unemployment area incentives is further reduced when we consider that urban location costs are 7-11 percent *higher* than rural costs. However, this estimate does not allow for the higher transportation cost associated with rural locations.

The economically distressed area incentives reduce costs by 2 percent for most firms, and by 4 percent for the larger ones. Thus, they may have an impact, but *only* in the minority of cases under assumptions regarding excluded costs that are most favorable to urban areas.

The combined package of incentives will, of course, give the largest reduction in urban location costs. This reduction will be 3-5 percent. This may in many cases be sufficient to compensate a firm for expanding in the city as opposed to the suburbs or a non-metropolitan area.

Given that the Urban Jobs Program represents one of the newest and most comprehensive locational subsidy programs designed to stimulate development in depressed areas, these results do not bode well for similar programs across the country. Two of the three incentive packages appear not to reduce urban location costs sufficiently to compensate for the basic cost disadvantages of these communities, with the combined package offering more substantial subsidies. This should not be surprising, since in developing the UJP there was no attempt to estimate the actual cost of production differences between different parts of the state.

With incentives that will provide sufficient benefits to firms in a limited number of cases, unless the state is very careful most of the companies availing themselves of the subsidies will be making investments they would be making anyway. The state recognizes this problem but has not established eligibility criteria capable of solving it. To qualify for the job grant, a firm must merely notify the Department of Economic Development while an expansion is in the planning stage. To qualify for the tax incentives, a firm only has to show that it has expanded employment.

Where state multi-family housing finance programs have been targeted to distressed communities, they have been plagued by some of the same problems as the Urban Jobs Program. To cause multi-family housing to be developed in a distressed community, the lack of effective demand must be overcome. In short, something must be done to compensate for the fact that people there cannot afford to pay market rents. By subsidizing housing construction costs through below market rate financing, the state housing agency attempts to compensate the developer for the low rents they must charge to fill the units. Often this interest subsidy only amounts to the difference between the taxable borrowing rate and the tax-exempt borrowing rate, a cost break that *cannot* sufficiently reduce rents for many moderate and low income families. Either the housing does not get built in depressed areas or it is filled by relatively well-off renters.

The more successful state programs to promote multi-family housing for distressed areas have made use of additional federal and state subsidies. For example, the Massachusetts Housing Finance Agency (MHFA) has built only 29 percent of its housing in suburban areas—with 60 percent in urban sites and 11 percent in rural sites. And 38 percent of this housing is occupied by low income families; moderate income families occupy another 54 percent.

THE SPECIAL PROBLEM OF RETAINING MATURE FIRMS

While we have emphasized business start-ups and expansions in developing a healthy local economy, communities should not ignore opportunities to prevent the shutdown of existing, mature businesses. Even though these plant closings represent a relatively small component of overall unemployment, they produce especially pernicious effects (Gilman, 1979). Those employees laid off permanently when a plant shuts down tend to be out of work for comparatively long periods and to experience relatively large earnings reductions when re-employed. And when the closing firm is a major employer, it means substantial lost tax revenues and negative multiplier effects that signal a community-wide disaster.

Although these lost jobs might be replaced by new businesses or expansions, it is unlikely that they will match perfectly the skills of the laid-off workers. More importantly, saving endangered plants may frequently be a cost effective way of "creating" jobs. In the first case, plant closings sometimes represent essentially profitable operations that have not been managed properly. Often this involves a conglomerate being out of touch with one of its local divisions, or imposing excessive overhead and unfair internal pricing on the plant. Such was the case with the Saratoga Knitting Mill in Saratoga Springs, N.Y., whose sales began plummeting when its conglomerate parent tried to merge the firm's marketing force with that of another division. Under circumstances of this type, far from having to prop up a non-competitive business, a community simply needs to effect a transfer of ownership to people who can run the firm efficiently. After an employee-community coalition bought Saratoga Knitting Mills and restored a sound marketing operation, the firm's profits soared.

In the other case, the plant may in fact not be profitable when compared to other investment opportunities of similar risk that the owners' have available to them. This is probably the case with the vast majority of plant deaths or relocations. But the operation may be very far from being in the red. Such was the case for the Library Bureau, Inc. in Herkimer, N.Y., a manufacturer of library furniture owned by Sperry Rand. When the parent corporation decided to liquidate Library Bureau, the firm was earning a 13 percent pre-tax return on equity. This fell far short of the 22 percent pre-tax return that Sperry Rand demanded of its operations. But as Congressman Peter Kostmeyer, a leader in the movement to deal with plant closings, points out in discussing situations of this type, "Very often the plant could be continued at a profit which is acceptable to an employee or resident-employee ownership group, while maintaining the jobs which are vital to that community." Under these circumstances, an employee or residents' group must coalesce and buy the plant; failing that, some public entity must be willing to subsidize the enterprise to the point of making it attractive for conventional investors. This latter option should not be pursued if it would cost more than equivalent job creation through promoting start-ups or expansions. In the case of Library Bureau, Inc., employees and community residents successfully bought out Sperry Rand, saving 270 jobs.

For a successful buy-out to occur, several ingredients must be present. These ingredients range from sufficient advance warning that the plant will be shut down, to technical and managerial expertise on the part of those groups interested in purchasing the operation. For purposes of this study, we want to focus on the availability of capital for those parties interested in taking over the firm. Capital needs will be of two types. There must be the actual long-term capital available with which to acquire the firm from its current owners. In addition, there may be a need for "bridge financing" to keep the operation going from the time the owners decide to close down until the buyers have obtained long-term financing and finalized the deal.

Those parties attempting to raise funds for a buy-out—whether they be individual entrepreneurs, employee groups or community coalitions—will face all the market imperfections described in previous chapters. Besides pursuing a relatively small venture in most cases, the purchasing parties will likely be perceived by lenders as wanting to operate an enterprise that the current owners found less than adequate. Add to this prejudice against employee or worker ownership where that is the form of acquisition, and the product is a significant capital gap. Reports Andrew Field, financial strategist for the Vermont asbestos miners who bought out their failing employer: "When we went to the big lenders their first reaction was, 'Jesus Christ, the monkeys are going to run the zoo?'" (Zwerdling, 1979.)

Ultimately the Vermont asbestos miners got a loan, but only through a 100 percent guarantee provided by the Vermont Industrial Development Authority. The case represented the exception rather than the rule, however. State development finance efforts have not been geared to facilitating buy-outs of enterprises about to shutdown. Legislation now being considered in states around the country may be a first step toward rectifying this situation. Bills regulating certain aspects of plant closings have been introduced in nine states. Three of these bills—those in Michigan, New York and Oregon—provide for assistance in financing an acquisition, although the provisions are very general.

MAXIMIZING THE BENEFITS OF DEPRESSED AREA DEVELOPMENT

Developing job opportunities in depressed areas will not, by itself, ensure that unemployed or low income people benefit from them. Consider the experience of two firms in the black Roxbury section of Boston. Stride Rite, a major shoe manufacturer, has its oldest plant in Roxbury. While the community is not a competitive location for new Stride Rite capacity, the existing plant is fully paid for and depreciated, so it continues to operate until simply wearing out or becoming completely obsolete. With a current labor force of 487, it is one of the largest employers in Roxbury. However, residents of the community hold very few of these jobs. Of the factory and warehouse employees, Roxbury residents only make up 9 percent. A new branch plant of Digital Equipment, Inc. will soon be opening in the community largely as the result of public land assembly assistance. But while the Digital plant will be employing 300, the firm estimates that only 20 percent will be local residents.

So although the presence of jobs in a community will increase the employment chances of residents, the majority of positions may go to people from other areas. This argues for targeting beyond geographical areas to specific types of individuals who, because of income level, employment status, race, or other personal characteristics, are deemed most worthy of assistance.

One method for "people targeting" would be to further restrict the kind of firms eligible for market-correcting capital availability programs. We have already outlined how and why such programs can be restricted to firms starting up or operating in certain depressed geographical areas. Unfortunately, one reason enterprises which are operating in depressed areas often do not hire solely from the local labor pool, or from those most in need of work, is that these applicants have less education, fewer skills, and insufficient work experience. Hiring them *may* mean higher unit labor costs. In that case, requiring local residents to be hired can impose such added costs on an enterprise that it will no longer be sufficiently profitable. Thus a program designed to make capital available to underfinanced but competitive ventures may find itself with no investment opportunities if it requires these hiring practices. This will not be a problem if local workers are not being hired simply due to pure discrimination.

An alternative method for people targeting would be to offer financial incentives for hiring workers with certain characteristics. These would serve to compensate enterprises for the added costs of employing such individuals. Incentives could be combined with requirements that a firm's labor force include those deemed most in need of employment.

Whom a depressed area firm should hire is only one example of an important social cost or benefit which a state government may want to take account of in the development process. Jobs created through development are not all the same. Part of the dynamism of small firms comes as a result of greater innovativeness and entrepreneurial drive. But another part results from the greater ease with which employees can be let go, poorer working conditions, and lower pay and benefits (Gordon, 1979). The Birch data referred to in Chapter 1 show that while small firms as a whole generate most jobs, a large number go out of business soon after start-up. Employment for any individual worker in this sector may not be very secure. So there may be a significant trade-off between the number of jobs created and their quality. Nevertheless, states have only recently begun to confront the need for a capability to make systematic decisions about which of these costs and benefits are important, and how to minimize or maximize them.

A basic issue is that all private enterprises will ignore costs and benefits external to them, in the absence of regulatory or political sanctions. Policymakers at the state level can try to assess and respond to social considerations by promulgating regulations or offering carrot and stick incentives to the enterprises who would otherwise ignore the externalities. An example of this approach occurs when a state legislature decides to compensate certain businesses if they operate in an economically distressed area.

The Role of Community-Based Organizations

Once a decision has been made to encourage investment in depressed regions, having institutions at the state level placing all kinds of conditions on firms receiving capital may not be the most effective way of dealing with externalities and equity considerations. This may be more appropriately the role of local, community-based organizations. After all, the residents of the community in which a venture is located bear many of its external effects. They have a strong incentive to respond to the social benefits of reduced crime and health problems resulting from lower unemployment, or to the social costs of environmental degradation. To the extent a venture must answer to its community, it will also be responsive to these impacts in operating and investment decisions.

This approach of making community-based organizations partners in the development finance process has been endorsed, in part, through the federal government's Special Impact Program (SIP) operated by the Community Services Administration (CSA). The Special Impact Program, rather than directly subsidizing or investing in business and housing ventures in depressed areas, makes capital grants to community-controlled, non-profit organizations known as Community Development Corporations (CDCs). CDCs invest this money in their wholly-owned enterprises, or in jointly owned ones initiated by local entrepreneurs. There are now approximately 44 SIP-funded CDCs, but the National Commission on Neighborhoods estimates that an additional 650 community-based economic development organizations exist, relying on a combination of foundation, federal agency, and state and local financing.

For CDCs to promote development in depressed areas that both produces jobs and effectively maximizes total benefits for local residents, four key ingredients must be present. First, the CDC itself must be truly representative and accountable to its community. Second, the CDC must be able to exercise influence over major business decisions of the ventures in which it invests. Third, it must have the technical expertise to develop ventures, on its own or with other investors. Fourth, the CDC must have the right kind of financing available to it from public or private sources. If the CDC ventures require subsidies to be viable, and insufficient ones are being provided through other mechanisms—wage subsidies, for example—this capital must be at below market cost.

Evaluating the CDC Record

Efforts to evaluate CDC experience have been rife with methodological problems, so we cannot give a simple summation of how successful they have been as partners in the development finance process. Their record has been far from perfect. In the absence of active community participation, some have turned into either minor business operations or political and economic tools of a few individuals. Lack of technical and managerial expertise has meant that the most successful ventures are often jointly owned with private entrepreneurs and thus less accountable to the CDC. Many CDC ventures have failed, indicating that free capital grants for early business financing will often not sufficiently compensate for the higher costs and inadequate markets present in depressed areas.

Despite instances of failure, financing economic development through CDCs has led to enough success stories as to suggest these institutions merit a greater role in the development finance process. One positive case study is the highly successful Kentucky Highlands Investment Corporation, whose operations we have described previously. And while KHIC has behaved much like a convention venture capitalist in the process, it does have some important differences. Most of its twenty-one policy making board of directors represents the community-based organizations that founded Kentucky Highlands. In screening venture proposals, it considers not just the expected profitability of a business but how it will benefit local residents as well. They would not, for example, help finance a highly capital-intensive chemical plant that required $10 million to build and was operated by a small staff. When KHIC does invest in a joint venture with a private entrepreneur, it receives a voice in the operation's decisions through a seat on its board of directors or other provisions. So far these firms have a strong record of hiring disadvantaged workers—a large majority of their employees were on unemployment or welfare before being hired. Beyond this business activity, KHIC has used its organizational resources and money to create facilities for community meetings, a child care facility for working mothers, and a nascent health maintenance organization (HMO).

KHIC is not entirely unique either. To the south, in Mississippi, the Delta Foundation CDC has used a similar venture capital approach to create several hundred jobs.

While KHIC and other CDCs have promoted several successful joint ventures, they have also started viable, wholly owned businesses. Community Products, Inc., a venture of the Hough Area Development Corporation in Cleveland, is one. Begun in 1969, CPI produces injection moulded rubber parts for the auto industry. The firm employs 60 people, of which 90 percent are from the Hough ghetto and two thirds are women. This work force includes many single parents who formerly received Aid for Dependent Children. It is estimated that at least 60 percent of the female employees would otherwise be on unemployment.

CPI, like most CDC ventures, would not exist if it were dependent on private capital that demanded a normal rate of return. Until 1974, the firm operated at a loss, then broke even for two years, and in 1976 began generating moderate profits. The difference between the firm's earnings and the expected returns required of an operation with its level of risk represents the implicit subsidy provided. But the savings in social welfare expenditures alone that are attributable to CPI's existence would appear to make up for this subsidy.

Besides starting up new businesses, Community Development Corporations have been active in salvaging firms ready to close down. A good example of this effort is the Harlem Commonwealth Council's purchase of Schultz Manufacturing Company. Schultz's parent company, National Industries, planned to close the firm in 1972 because its return did not match other opportunities the conglomerate faced. So HCC, founded in 1967 and funded by the Special Impact Program, bought Schultz from National Industries for $900,000, with $600,000 in equity coming from CSA and a $300,000 SBA-guaranteed long-term loan from Citicorp Venture Capital, Ltd. The company now employs approximately 120 people. Moreover, though prior to HCC's acquisition of Schultz most of the labor force came from outside Harlem, this distribution has been reversed. While the firm's profits have been substantial—for example, a 12 percent pre-tax return on equity in 1977—like Community Products, Inc. it would not exist if a normal return were required.

Perhaps housing development provides the clearest contrast of how community-based organizations employ subsidized capital as compared to conventional investors. Take the 504-unit Nueva Maravilla Housing Project developed by The East Los Angeles Community Union (TELACU), a CDC. In designing and building the project, it gave major planning responsibility to a council of Maravilla area residents. They produced a housing development that includes recreation, health care and social service facilities. In addition, TELACU obtained a manpower training grant during construction so they could train local residents to work on the building crews. Today Neuva Maravilla stands as a model housing development when compared to other publicly developed housing around the country.

Or consider Lower Roxbury Community Corporation's Madison Park III 120-unit housing development in Boston. Like most CDC housing ventures, it was done in partnership with private developers. However, LRCC delayed bringing these developers into a partnership for quite some time, even at a financial loss to itself, until it was in a position to assert control over the quality of the project: "There was a great fear of letting control reside in the hands of the limited partners due to the fact that these investors were buying in primarily for the tax losses to shield other income. Since the cash flow from the operation of these projects was of relative insignificance, there was no incentive to run viable projects that would provide high quality housing (the rapid deterioration of housing built under Sec. 236 program due to this phenomenon confirms this fear)" (Rubin, 1978).

In addition to the economic-related benefits described above, making community-based organizations partners in the development finance process confers a political benefit on depressed communities that is unlikely to be achieved in any other way. Control over economic resources has always had a degree of political power associated with it, and this is as true for community organizations as it is for private investors. For example, TELACU has developed substantial political clout in the California Democratic Party, and its members have been appointed to several state and local positions. Pointing out the sources of this influence, the state Democratic Party chief stated, "They have certainly succeeded in their economic development efforts, and this has had tremendous ripple effects in the political arena" (*California Journal,* 1979).

State Capital Assistance for Community-Based Development

A recent survey of state government support for community-based development efforts turned up very little activity (Center for Community Economic Development, 1978). Only two states have programs of any kind that are explicitly designed to channel capital into CDC-managed development. Of equal importance, there is virtually no evidence that states have given special attention to these organizations in their regular capital assistance programs.

The two CDC-oriented state programs do illustrate the issues that will be faced in designing and implementing such an assistance policy. In 1975, Minnesota began a modestly funded Minnesota Community Corporation Act, modeled on the federal Special Impact Program. MCDC provides both planning and venture *grants* to eligible community based development organizations. For example, it gave $75,000 to the Chippewa Indian Tribe which was used to leverage an additional $434,000 for a cattle ranch operation.

A larger, though still modest, program is Massachusetts' Community Development Finance Corporation (CDFC), established in 1976 and operating since 1978. Rather than make outright grants, CDFC makes investments in CDC-controlled business ventures in depressed areas. It will emphasize equity investment as opposed to debt, receiving its return in the form of capital gains. The institution cannot hold more than 49 percent of total equity in a venture. For a venture to be eligible, several conditions must be met. The sponsoring CDC must allow all area residents to be members, and this membership must directly elect a majority of the CDC's board. The business venture must be subject to the CDC's control, through substantial ownership or the right to approve major business transactions. The legislation further requires that the financed ventures "increase or maintain primary employment"—full-time year-round work that pays at least one and a half times the minimum wage and provides adequate fringe benefits. CDFC's own financing was described in Chapter 6.

In the early going CDFC has run up against several problems. Its requirement relating to the political structure of eligible CDCs, intended to keep out organizations with no community base, may be too stringent—eliminating many legitimate groups. The absence of any resources for helping community groups to identify venture opportunities and develop business plans has hamstrung CDFC; it was as if KHIC had not had the aid of Venture Founders. This has been partly rectified with the legislature's establishment of the Community Economic Development Assistance Corporation (CEDAC).

The key long-run challenge for CDFC and like efforts will be their sources of funds. Without doubt there are many potential community-based ventures that can pay market rates for their capital, which in turn could enable a state financial intermediary like CDFC to raise its funds in the general capital markets. Conventional investors do not finance these community-based firms now because of various market imperfections, particularly discrimination against innovative organizational forms. But the number of these competitive ventures will be relatively limited when compared to the need for jobs. This is especially true when one considers any additional costs these firms will have to absorb in ensuring high quality jobs. Community-based firms will already face the challenge of operating in higher cost, economically distressed areas. These facts mean that a serious, long-term commitment to a community-based development strategy will entail providing deep subsidies, including but not limited to capital *grants*. To provide these subsidies, state governments would need to increase progressive taxation as well as possibly impose tax-like asset flow regulations on private financial institutions. At this point there is neither the will nor ability for any individual state government to move in this direction.

BIBLIOGRAPHY

Aaronson, J. and Schwartz, E., "Financing Public Goods and the Distribution of Population in a System of Local Governments," *National Tax Journal*, June 1973.

Advisory Commission on Intergovernmental Relations, *Interregional and Interstate Tax Competition*, May 18, 1979.

―――, *State-Local Taxation and Industrial Location, Report A-30*, Government Printing Office, Washington, D.C., 1967.

―――, *Taxation*, Government Printing Office, Washington, D.C., 1963.

Allaman, P. and D. Birch, *Working Papers #1-8, Inter-Area Migration Project*, Joint Center for Urban Studies of M.I.T. and Harvard, 1975.

Alsop, R. "Property-Tax Breaks for Firms Proliferate, But Need Is Disputed," *Wall Street Journal*, June 30, 1978.

Alonso, W., "Metropolis Without Growth," *The Public Interest*, Fall 1978.

Bartz, L., et al., *An Analysis of Digital Equipment Company's Decision to Locate a Branch Plant in the Crosstown Industrial Park*, unpublished manuscript, Department of City and Regional Planning, Harvard University, January 1979.

Benston, G. "The Optimal Banking Structure: Theory and Evidence," *Current Perspectives in Banking*, Thomas Havrilesky and John Boorman, eds. AHM Publishing Corp., Arlington Heights, Illinois, 1976.

Birch, D., *The Job Generation Process*, M.I.T. Program on Neighborhood and Regional Change, 1979.

―――, "The Processes Causing Economic Change in Cities," prepared for the Department of Commerce Conference on Business Retention and Expansion, 1978.

―――, "Regional Differences in Factor Costs: Labor, Land, Capital and Transportation," paper presented at conference in Austin, Texas, September 1977.

Bradford, D. and H. Kelejian, "An Econometric Model of the Flight to the Suburbs," *Journal of Political Economy*, Vol. 81, No. 3, May/June 1973.

Brealy, R. and S. Myers, *Principles of Corporate Finance*, manuscript to be published by McGraw Hill, 1979.

Bureau of National Affairs, "State Housing Agencies," *Housing and Development Reporter*, 1979.

Business Week, "Keeping Small Business in Town," July 17, 1978.

Business Week, "SEC Help for Small Companies," May 7, 1979.

CSBS (Conference of State Bank Supervisors). *A Profile of State Chartered Banking*, 1977.

California Journal, "Lizarraga and TELACU—Hispanic Political Leaders at Last?" October 1979.

Center for Community Economic Development, "Community Economic Development and the States," Cambridge, Massachusetts, 1978.

Chandross, R., "The Impact of New Bank Entry on Unit Banks in One Bank Towns," *Journal of Bank Research,* Autumn 1973.

Chinitz, B., "Toward a National Urban Policy," undated manuscript.

Coe, C., "State Supervision and Assistance in Local Government Financial Management," State Government, Summer 1978.

Cohen, et al., *Residential Fuel Policy and the Environment,* Ballinger Books, Cambridge, 1974.

The Conference Board, "Household Savings," *Road Maps of Industry,* No. 1805, April 1977.

Cornia, et al., *State-Local Fiscal Incentives and Economic Development,* Academy for Contemporary Problems, Columbus, Ohio, June 1978.

Daniels, B., "Models and Options for the Alaska Permanent Funds Functions, Regionalization, and Accountability," unpublished manuscript, September 1977.

———, *The Relevance of European Development Finance to North American Economic Development,* working paper, Department of City and Regional Planning, Harvard, Cambridge, January 1978.

———, and M. Kieschnick, *A Policy Primer on Development Finance, Parts I-III,* paper for the National Policy Project on Development Finance, March 1979.

——— and ———, *Theory and Practice in the Design of Development Finance Innovation,* working paper, Department of City and Regional Planning, Harvard University, Cambridge, November 1978.

———, and S. Pfifferling, *The Impact of State Economic Development Strategies on Urban Neighborhoods,* report for the National Commission on Neighborhoods, October 1978.

Day, K., et al., *New L.I.F.E.: A Private Sector-Initiated Market Innovation,* unpublished manuscript, Department of City and Regional Planning, Harvard University, Cambridge, 1979.

Economic Development Administration, *Survey of Industrial Location Determinants,* U.S. Department of Commerce, Washington, D.C., 1971.

Federal Trade Commission, *Mergers and Acquisitions,* 1978.

Forbes, R. and J. Petersen, *Building a Broader Market,* McGraw Hill, New York, 1976.

Fraser, D. and P. Rose, "Bank Entry and Bank Performance," *Journal of Finance,* March 1972.

Gambs, M., "Bank-Failures—An Historical Perspective," *Monthly Review,* Federal Reserve Bank of Kansas City, June 1977.

Gardner, C., *Banking Regulation and Urban Growth,* the Rand Corporation, P-5057, July 1973.

Gilbert, R., "Effectiveness of State Reserve Requirements," *Monthly Review,* Federal Reserve Bank of St. Louis, September 1978.

Gilman, H., *The Economic Costs of Worker Dislocation: An Overview,* prepared for a conference sponsored by the National Commission for Employment Policy, July 1979.

Gleisser, B., et al., *First Year Assessment of the Massachusetts Capital Resource Company*, unpublished manuscript, Department of City and Regional Planning, Harvard University, Cambridge, January 1979.

Glen, M., "Tax-Free Bonds for Housing—Too Good to Be True?" *National Journal*, April 28, 1979.

Gordon, D., *The Working Poor*, Council of State Planning Agencies, Washington, D.C., 1979.

Gravelle, J. and D. Kiefer, "The Investment Tax Credit: An Analytical Overview, Report No. 79-77E," Congressional Research Service, Library of Congress, March 1979.

Grebler, L., "An Assessment of the Performance of the Public Sector on the Residential Housing Market: 1955-74," in *Capital Markets and the Housing Sector*, ed. Buckley, et al., Ballinger, Cambridge, 1977.

Greenwood, M.J. "Urban Economic Growth and Migration: Their Interaction." *Environment and Planning*, January, 1973.

Griggs, J. and W. Petty, "Loan Practices of Commercial Banks and Economic Agglomeration," Economic Development Administration, September 1970.

Gumpert, D.E. "Venture Capital Becoming More Widely Available," *Harvard Business Review*, Jan.-Feb. 1979.

Haar, C. and P. Lewis, "Where Shall the Money Come From?" *Public Interest*, Winter 1970.

Harnett, H., "Industrial Climate in Central Cities," *American Industrial Development Conference Journal*, Vol. 7, No. 2, April 1972.

Harrison, B. and S. Kantor, "The Political Economy of State Job-Creation Business Incentives," *Journal of the American Institute of Planners*, October 1978.

_____. and _____. "The Great State Robbery," *Working Papers for a New Society*, Spring 1976.

Heggestad, A., "Market Structure, Risk and Profitability in Commercial Banking," *Journal of Finance*, September 1977.

_____. "Market Structure, Competition, and Performance in Financial Industries: A Survey of Banking Studies," in *Issues in Financial Regulation*, ed. F. Edwards, McGraw-Hill, New York, 1979.

Horvitz, P. and B. Shull, "The Impact of Branching on Performance," *The National Banking Review*, 2, December 1964.

Horwitz, M., "Redlining as an Investment Strategy," *New York Times*, December 12, 1976.

Hovey, H., "Development Finance for Distressed Areas," draft report, Northeast Midwest Institute, Washington, D.C., January 1979.

_____, "State Urban Development Strategies," Council of State Planning Agencies, Washington, D.C., 1977.

Hyman, D., *The Economics of Government Activity*, Holt, Rinehart and Winston,

New York, 1973.

IILED (Institute of International Law and Economic Development), *The Industrial Revenue Bond as a Financial Attraction Device,* Economic Development Administration, Office of Economic Development, September 1978.

Izraeli, O., *Differentials in Nominal Incomes and Prices Between Cities,* Ph.D. dissertation, University of Chicago, 1973.

Kemper, P., *Manufacturing Location, Production Requirements, and Market Characteristics,* unpublished, 1974.

Kimball, R., "States as Financial Intermediaries," *New England Economic Review,* January/February 1976.

Kohn, E., "Branch Banking, Bank Mergers and the Public Interest," New York State Banking Department, 1964.

Korschot, B. "Prudent Investing Before and After ERISA," *Financial Analysis Journal,* July/August 1977.

Levin, S., "Suburban-Central City Property Tax Differentials and the Location of Industry: Some Evidence," *Land Economics,* Vol. 50, No. 4, November 1974.

Light, J., and W. White, *The Financial System,* Irwin, Inc., Homewood, Illinois, 1979.

Lynch, G. and W. Hardin, "Money Flows and Usury Ceilings; How Loanable Funds Left Arkansas in 1974," College of Business Administration, University of Arkansas, Little Rock, January 1979.

Maxwell and Aronson, *Financing State and Local Governments,* 2nd edition, Brookings Institute, Washington, 1977.

McCall, A. and M. Petersen, "The Impact of De Novo Commercial Bank Entry," *Journal of Finance,* December 1977.

MacEachen, et al., *Case Study: Stride Rite and Roxbury,* unpublished manuscript, Department of City and Regional Planning, Harvard University, January 1979.

Melton, W. and D. Heidt, "Variable Rate Mortgages," Federal Reserve Bank of New York, Summer 1979.

Minge, D., "Guarantying Municipal Bonds," *Wisconsin Law Review,* 1974:89, Number 1.

Moes, J., "Reply (to Goffman and Thompson)," *Southern Economic Journal,* October 1962.

Mullaney, T., "SEC's Fingers on Wall Street's Pulse," *New York Times,* May 3, 1978.

Muth, R., "Differential Growth Among Large U.S. Cities," in J. Quirk and A. Zarley, eds., *Papers in Quantitative Economics,* University of Kansas Press, 1968.

Nathan, R., *Lessons from European Experience for a U.S. Development Bank,* International Urban Reports, The Council for International Urban Liaison, January 1979.

National Association of Securities Dealers, Inc., *Small Business Financing: The Current Environment and Suggestions for Improvement,* Special Report, May 1979.

Olvey, L., "Regional Growth and Interregional Migration: Their Pattern of Interaction," *Review of Regional Studies,* Winter 1972.

Orr, L., *Income, Employment and Urban Residential Location,* Academic Press, New York, 1975.

Orren, K., *Corporate Power and Social Change,* Johns Hopkins University Press, Baltimore, Maryland, 1974.

Parliment, T., and J. Koden, *Usury Ceilings: The Threat to Housing,* Economic Working Paper, U.S. Savings and Loan Association, Chicago, January 1979.

Petersen, J., *The Rating Game,* Report of the Twentieth Century Fund Task Force on Municipal Bond Credit Ratings, 1974.

―――, "Small Borrowers: Does Size Matter?" National Conference on Nonmetropolitan Community Services Research, Columbus, Ohio, January 1977.

―――, et al., *Watching and Counting: A Survey of State Assistance to and Supervision of Local Government Debt and Financial Administration,* Municipal Finance Officers Association, 1977.

Philip, A., *Creating New Jobs: A Report on Long-Term Job Creation in Britain and Sweden,* Policy Studies Institute, London, England, 1978.

Pierce, N. and J. Hagstrom, "Aiding Entrepreneurs—A New Approach to the Old War on Poverty," *National Journal,* August 8, 1979.

Ransom, P., *Evaluation of Massachusetts Capital Resource Company's First Year,* Massachusetts Social and Economic Opportunity Council, May 1979.

Rout, L., "More Banks Offering Lower-Interest Loans to Small Businessmen," *Wall Street Journal,* March 5, 1979.

Rubin, D., "Lower Roxbury Corporation," in *Revitalizing Distressed Neighborhoods: Report to the Economic Development Task Force of the National Commission on Neighborhoods,* Department of City and Regional Planning, Harvard University.

Schmenner, R., "The Manufacturing Location Decision: Evidence from Cincinnati and New England," Economic Development Administration, Department of Commerce, March 1978.

Shafer, R., *Mortgage Lending Decisions: Criteria and Contrasts,* Harvard University, 1979 (unpublished).

Small Business Administration, *Report of the SBA Task Force on Venture and Equity Capital for Small Business,* 1977.

Smith, "Alternative Methods for Raising Capital: Rights vs. Underwritten Offerings," *Journal of Financial Economics,* December 1977.

Smith, L., "Tax-Free Housing Bonds Cost More Than They Are Worth," *Fortune,* July 2, 1979.

Steinnes, D., "Causality and Intraurban Location," *Journal of Urban Economics,* Vol. 4, No. 1, 1977.

Sternlieb, G. and J. Hughes, *Post-Industrial America: Metropolitan Decline and Interregional Job Shifts,* Center for Urban Policy Research, Rutgers, New-

Brunswick, New Jersey, 1975.

Stigler, G. "Imperfections in the Capital Market," *Journal of Political Economy*, June 1967.

Stone, D., *Industrial Location in Metropolitan Areas*, Praeger, New York, 1976.

Straszheim, M., "An Introduction and Overview of Regional Money Capital Markets," Economic Development Administration, Department of Commerce, 1969.

Sviekauskas, L.H., "The Productivity of Cities," *Quarterly Journal of Economics*, Vol. 89, No. 3, August 1975.

Talley, S., "Recent Trends in Local Banking Market Structure," Staff Economic Studies, Board of Governors of the Federal Reserve System, 1977.

Thompson, W. and J. Mattila, *An Econometric Model of Post-War State Industrial Development*. Wayne State University Press, 1959.

Thurow, L., in *Policies for a More Competitive Financial System*, Conference Series No. 8, Federal Reserve Bank of Boston.

Timbers, Stephen, "The Non-Efficient Market is not for Institutional Investors," *Journal of Portfolio Management*, 1977.

Ujakovich, R., "The Connecticut Urban Jobs Program—Expected Effects and Recommendations for Restructuring," unpublished manuscript, Kennedy School of Government, Harvard University, April 1979.

U.S. Bureau of Census, *Statistical Abstract of the United States*, Washington, D.C., 1978.

U.S. Bureau of Census, *Statistical Abstract of the United States*, Washington, D.C., 1977.

U.S. Bureau of Census, *Statistical Abstract of the United States*, Washington, D.C., 1974.

U.S. Internal Revenue Service, *Statistics of Income, Corporation Income Tax Returns*, annual.

University of Georgia, *State Laws Governing Local Government Structure and Administration*, Institute of Government, March 1978.

Vaughan, R., *State Taxation and Economic Development*, Council of State Planning Agencies, Washington, D.C., 1979.

Vaughan, R., *The Urban Impacts of Federal Policies: Vol. 2*, the Rand Corporation, R-2028-KF/RC, June 1977.

Verbrugge, J., *Tax-Exempt Bonds for Single-Family Housing: An Evaluation of State Housing Finance Agency and Local Government Programs*, Committee on Banking, Finance and Urban Affairs, House of Representatives, Hearings, 1979.

West, R., "Brokers' Fortunes Since 'May Day,'" *Wall Street Journal*, 191:20, November 24, 1978.

Wheat, L., *Regional Growth and Industrial Location*, Lexington Books, 1973.

Zwerdling, D., "Employee Ownership - How Well Is It Working?" *Working Papers for a New Society*, May/June 1979.

STUDIES IN STATE DEVELOPMENT POLICY

Please send me the following publications:

Quantity	Title	No.	Price	Total
_____	*State Taxation and Economic Development*	3614	$9.95	_____
_____	*Economic Development: The Challenge of the 1980s*	3610	$9.95	_____
_____	*Innovations in Development Finance*	3612	$9.95	_____
_____	*The Working Poor*	3611	$8.95	_____
_____	*Inflation and Unemployment*	3618	$8.95	_____
_____	*Democratizing the Development Process*	3616	$7.95	_____
_____	*Venture Capital and Urban Development*	3613	$8.95	_____
_____	*Development Politics: Private Development and the Public Interest*	3617	$8.95	_____
_____	*The Capital Budget*	3615	$8.95	_____
	TOTAL ORDER			_____

☐ Payment enclosed (no charge for handling and postage)

☐ Please bill me (postage and $2 handling charge will be added)

Payment must accompany all orders under $20.

Name: _____

Title: _____

Address: _____

_____

City, State, Zip _____

Make checks payable to the Council of State Planning Agencies.

Important Note: Discounts of 10% are available on any order of four or more titles. A discount of 20% is available to individuals and institutions ordering the entire nine-volume series ($60.00 per set). Full payment must accompany requests for discounts.